Cover image: *Mandala of the Five Elements*. This is a copy of a 16th century Nepalese painting. The mandala was used as a diagnostic and healing tool in Ayurvedic medicine. Painted by Ruth Perini (Srimukti) 2121.

ISBN: 978-0-6489107-7-0

Dedication

To the next generation

Olli, Arlo and Gangotri

Yoga Upanishad Series *Volume 7*

Trishikhi-Brahmanopanishad

Attaining Yoga

Original Sanskrit text with

Transliteration, Translation

and Commentary

by **Ruth Perini (Srimukti)**

CONTENTS

Introduction		1
Invocation		8

First Text

Verses

1-2.	Brāhmanam	9
3-4.	How the World Was Formed	12
5.	Five Elements	14
6.	Functions of the Elements	16
7.	Tanmātra	18
8.	Deities of the Twelve Nāḍīs	19
9.	Synthesis of the Five Elements	21

Second Text

1-4a.	Division & Combination of the Elements	24
4b-5.	What the World Consists Of	26
6-8.	Forms of the Elements	28
9.	Ātman at Sahasrāra	30
10-11.	Four States of Consciousness	31
12-13.	Koṣa	33
14-15.	Renunciation	35
16-18.	Satsang	37
19-23.	Yoga and Jñāna	39
24-28a.	Twofold Yoga	42
28b-32a.	Eightfold Path	45
32b-34a.	Yama and Niyama	48
34b-40.	Āsana: Svastika Gomukha Vīra Padma	51
41-46.	Āsana: Kukkuta Kūrma Dhanur Bhadra Mukta	57
47-52.	Āsana: Māyūra Matsya Siddha Paścimottāna Sukha	61
53-55.	Prāṇāyāma	66
56-57.	Region of Fire	68
58-62.	Place of the Jīva	70
63-65.	Kuṇḍalinī	73
66-69.	Centre of the Body	76

70-76.	Eight Nāḍīs	78
72-82.	Ten Vital Airs	81
83-89a.	Functions of the Vital Airs	84
89b-91.	Place of Sādhana	87
92-94.	Posture for Prāṇāyāma	89
95-101.	Nāḍī Śodhana Leads to Kumbaka	92
102-104a.	Benefits of Prāṇāyāma (1)	97
104b-110.	Benefits of Prāṇāyāma (2)	99
111-113.	Benefits of Prāṇāyāma (3)	103
114-117.	Ṣaṇmukhī Mudrā	105
118-120.	Iḍā, Piṅgalā and Suṣumnā	108
121-129a	Signs of Approaching Death	110
129b-134	Pratyāhāra Leads to Dhāraṇā	114
135-145a	Meditation on the Five Elements	117
145b-149a	Meditating on Vāsudeva	124
149b-152a	States of Awareness	127
152b-156a	Meditation on Viṣṇu and the Universe	130
156b-165	Attaining Kaivalya	132

APPENDICES

A.	End Notes	137
B.	References	140
C.	Pronunciation Guide	142
D.	Sanskrit Text	144
E.	Continuous Translation	160
F.	Swami Satyadharma	176
G.	Author's Note	180

Introduction

Veda is a Sanskrit word meaning 'knowledge'. In the context of the Vedas, it means 'revealed knowledge which is *śruti*, 'heard' from within, not taught. These ancient spiritual texts or hymns, through which we can learn much of the perceptions and insights of the early vedic seers, are grouped into four *samhitas* or collections: *Rig Veda, Yajur Veda, Sāma Veda* and *Atharva Veda*. They were revealed to enlightened beings 3,000 to 4,500 years ago or more (the Rig-Veda contains astronomical references describing occurrences in 5,000 to 3,000 BCE), and transmitted orally by the sages from generation to generation within brahmin families.

The four Vedas were considered to be divine revelations, and each word was carefully memorised. This was to ensure accurate transmission, but also because each syllable was considered to have spiritual power, its source being the supreme, eternal sound. This was a mammoth task, as there are 20,358 verses in the four Vedas, approximately two thousand printed pages. They were composed in fifteen different metres, which demanded perfect control of the breath. Georg Feuerstein describes them as 'a composite of symbol, metaphor, allegory, myth and story, as well as paradox and riddle' and their composers as 'recipients and revealers of the invisible order of the cosmos [with] inspired insights or illumined visions'1.

Rig Veda

The Rig Veda is the oldest spiritual text in the world and still regarded as sacred, containing 1,028 hymns or songs of 10,589 verses in praise of the divine (*rig* or *ric* meaning 'praise'). Each hymn is recognised as a *mantra*, a sacred sound vibration, which releases energy from limited material awareness, thus expanding the consciousness. It is also the earliest surviving form of Sanskrit. The illumined seers composed the hymns while established in the highest consciousness, thus able to commune with luminous beings of the higher realms. There are about 250 hymns in praise of *Indra*, the divine force behind the ocean, heavens, thunder, lightning, rain and the light of the sun; 200 of *Agni*, born of the Sun, becoming the god of sacrificial fire, and over 100 of *Soma*, who gives immortality, and who is connected to the Sun, Moon, mountains, rivers and oceans. Others are dedicated to *Varuna*, who protects cosmic order; the *Ashvins*, supreme healers; *Ushas*, goddess of the dawn; *Aditi*, goddess of eternity; and *Saraswati*, goddess of the Vedas and of music and the arts.

Yajur Veda

The hymns of the Yajur-Veda, Veda of Sacrifice, consist of sacrificial formulas or prayers, including those of an internal or spiritual nature, which are chanted by the *adhvaryu* (priest), who performs the sacrifice. About a third of its 1,975 verses are taken from the Rig Veda. The rest are original and in prose form.

Sāma Veda

The Sāma Veda, Veda of Chants, gives instructions on the chanting of vedic hymns. The majority of its 1,875 verses are from the Rig Veda; only 75 verses are original. Many of the hymns were sung by special priests during sacrificial rites. Some are still sung today.

Atharva Veda

The Atharva Veda, named after the seer Atharvan, whose family were great seers in vedic times, contains 731 hymns of 5,977 verses, about one fifth of which are from the RigVeda. Much of the Atharva Veda consists of magical spells and charms for gaining health, love, peace and prosperity, or taking revenge on an enemy. Possibly for this reason, the Atharva Veda was either not accepted by the orthodox priesthood, or not given the same standing as the other Vedas.

The vedic people and their culture

The vedic people lived for over 2,500 years mainly along the banks of the Saraswati River, which was located in Northern India between the modern Ravi and Yamuna Rivers down to what is now the desert of Rajasthan. The Saraswati River dried up in about 1,900 BCE due to tectonic upheavals. Other areas of habitation included the Ganges River and its tributaries, rivers in Afghanistan (previously called Gandhara), the Himalayas and Mount Kailash in Tibet.

The vedic people had a complex multi-tiered view of the universe, in which humankind, nature and the divine are intertwined and interrelated. They had a deep knowledge of the oceans, mountains, deserts and forests of the physical world, as well as of the subtle worlds of deities and different levels of consciousness. People lived in cities or villages or were nomads, and were fully engaged in worldly life. They were an agrarian people, yet also had herds of cattle, horses and camels. Cities were constructed of stone, bricks and metal. They built chariots and ships. They were skilled workers in gold, metal, clay, stone, wood, leather and wool, and showed a very high standard in arts, crafts, astrology, medicine, music, dance and poetry.

After the Vedas

The Vedas were the foundation for the later revelations (*śruti*) in the *Brāhmaṇas* (ritual texts), the *Āranyakas* (texts on rituals and meditation for forest-dwelling ascetics) and the *Upaniṣads* (esoteric texts). Later still, the Vedas were the basis for numerous works of remembered or traditional knowledge, known as *smṛti,* including the epics: i.e. the *Mahābhārata, Rāmāyaṇa* and *Purāṇas,* and the *Sūtras,* or threads of knowledge, e.g. *Yoga Sūtras.* All these texts contain many concepts and practices, which come directly from the four Vedas.

Upaniṣads

The word *upaniṣad* is comprised of three roots: *upa* or 'near', *ni* or 'attentively', and *sad,* 'to sit'. The term describes the situation in which these unique texts were transmitted. The students or disciples sat near the realized master and listened attentively, as he expounded his experiences and understanding of the ultimate reality. These teachings are said to destroy the ignorance or illusion of the spiritual aspirant in regard to what is self and non-self, what is real and unreal, in relation to the absolute and relative reality. Only disciples were chosen, who had persevered in *sādhana catuṣṭaya*, the four kinds of spiritual effort, viz. *viveka* (discrimination between the permanent and impermanent), *vairagya* (non-attachment), *ṣadsampatti* (six virtues of serenity, self-control, withdrawal of the senses, endurance, perfect concentration and strong faith) and *mumukṣutva* (intense desire for liberation).

The Upaniṣads are derived from the Āranyakas, because they were chanted in the forest (*āranya*) after the aspirant had retired from worldly life. They are recorded in the later form of Sanskrit used in the Brāhmaṇas, and considered the last phase of *śruti*, vedic revelation. The Upaniṣads are regarded as *vedānta*, the end of the Vedas, inferring that *vedānta* is the end or completion of all perceivable knowledge, as they guide the aspirant beyond the limited mind to the *ātman* (spiritual self) and thus to *mokṣa* (liberation). Each upaniṣad reflected the teachings and tradition of a realized master, and was connected with a specific Veda and vedic school. It is estimated that there are over 200 Upaniṣads, which have been divided into seven groups: *Major*, *Vedānta*, *Śaiva, Śakta, Vaiśnava, Sannyasa* and *Yoga.*

Yoga Upaniṣads

The twenty-one Yoga Upaniṣads give an understanding of the hidden forces in nature and human beings, and describe esoteric yogic practices by which these forces can be manipulated and controlled. They emphasise that the inner journey to the one permanent reality, the *ātman*, is the essential one. Journeys to external places, such as holy sites and temples, as well as rituals and ceremonies, are not given importance. Their teachings give important information on the subtle body (*cakras, koṣas, prāṇa, kuṅḍalinī,* meditative states), and the tantric and yogic techniques, not given in the earlier upaniṣads, to attain them. Therefore, they are regarded as a significant integration of Vedanta and Tantra, which were previously considered incompatible. They are classified as 'minor' only because they postdate Adi Shankara.

Although their teachings actually predate Patañjali, the Yoga Upaniṣads were codified after the *Yoga Sūtras of Patañjali,* and form an important part of the classical yoga literature. However, they contain no references to Patañjali or his *Yoga Sūtras*. So, although the compilation of the Yoga Upaniṣads is post-Patañjali, the *vidyās*, or meditative disciplines, contained within them are pre-Patañjali. The Yoga Upaniṣads emerged at a time when the vedic and tantric cultures were coming together to share their knowledge. The wise thinkers from each culture sat down together and discussed how their insights and teachings could be combined in order to benefit humanity. Thus these upanisads combine the teachings of both tantra and yoga. It is evident in them that yoga leads to vedānta, and vedānta leads to yoga. However, they were written down by vedantic scholars and practitioners in order to show that these *vidyās* and related practices were not borrowed from Patañjali, but were known and practised from the ancient period.

Within the twenty-one Yoga Upaniṣads are six sub-groups which have their own main focus. The *Bindu Upaniṣads*, which include the *Amṛta-Bindu* (also known as the *Brahma-Bindu-Upaniṣad*), *Amṛta-Nada-Bindu*, *Nada-Bindu*, *Dhyāna-Bindu* and *Tejo-Bindu-Upaniṣads*, all concentrate on the bindu, the source or origin of all sound, and hence of creation. Bindu represents the transcendental sound manifested in the mantra *Aum*. The *Hamsa-Mantra, Soham*, is the main practice of the *Hamsa*, *Brahma-Vidya*, *Mahavakya* and *Paśupata-Brahma-Upaniṣads*. Concentration on *prāṇa*, the life force related to the process of inhalation and exhalation, brings the yogin to the knowledge of the transcendental self. The light of pure consciousness, which the enlightened irradiate, is the theme of the *Advaya-Taraka* and *Maṅḍala-Brahmana-Upaniṣads*. The *Kṣurika-Upaniṣad* (*kṣurika* meaning 'dagger') emphasises non-attachment as a means to liberation. The sixth group, comprised of eight late Yoga Upaniṣads from 1200 to 1300 A.D., covers teachings related to hatha and kundalini yogas. They are the *Yoga-Kuṅḍalī, Yoga-Tattwa, Yoga-Śikhā, Varāha, Śāndilya, Tri-Śikhi-Brahmana, Yoga-Darśana* and *Yoga-Chūdāmani Upaniṣads.*

Triśikhī-Brāhmaṇa-Upaniṣad

This Upaniṣad is related to the part of the Yajurveda called Śukla (white), meaning the verses are well-arranged and clear, and is said to belong to 14th or 15th century C.E.

A *brahmaṇa* with three tufts of hair (*triśikhī*), symbol of Śiva's trident, goes to *aditya-loka*, the world of the Sun to ask the fundamental questions of existence: "O Lord! What is the body? What is the breath? What is the cause? What is the soul?" The Sun replies that all comes from the form of Śiva, whose light is Brahman. From Brahman came the unmanifest, from which came the greater mind, from which came the individual form, from which came the five senses, from which came the five elements, from which came the entire world.

Then follows explanations of how the world was formed through the five major elements, their qualities, properties and functions, their synthesis and through *pañcikāraṇa*, the divisions and combinations of the elements. To return to the source, the unmanifest Brahman, the brahmaṇa should follow the eightfold path of yoga leading to *jñāna* and the path of *karmayoga* or *kriyāyoga*.

The necessity of renunciation and the importance of satsang, company of the wise, are emphasised. Each step of the eightfold path of yoga, viz. *yama, niyama, āsana, prāṇāyama, pratyāhāra, dhāraṇā, dhyāna and samādhi* is explained in detail. Comprehensive descriptions are given of the components of the subtle body, viz. *cakras, koṣas, nāḍīs, prāṇas, dhatus*, four states of consciousness kuṇḍalinī and *ātman*. Teachings are given on the *agni maṇḍala*, the region of fire and its role in awakening the subtle energies, and the *nāḍikanda*, where the three main *nāḍīs, iḍā piṅgalā* and *suṣumnā*, unite and separate. The practices and unique benefits of nāḍī śodhana and kumbhaka are described in detail. A peaceful solitary place in nature with fresh water and food nearby is recommended for progress in *sadhana*. One who has developed awareness of the prāṇas can recognise the signs of approaching death when the prāṇa reduces its flow to various parts of the body.

Practices for meditation: the five elements; the deities of the elements; Vāsudeva, the Transcendent Self; Viṣṇu; and the forms in the Universe. During meditation the *mudrās* held are *ṣaṇmukhī mudrā, hṛdayāñjali mudrā* or *khecarī mudrā* which help to channel the flow of prāṇa and awaken the dormant spiritual forces.

त्रिशिखी ब्राह्मणोपनिषद्
Triśikhī-Brāhmaṇopaniṣad

Opening Invocation

शान्तिपाठः
śāntipāṭhaḥ

ॐ पूर्णमिदः पूर्णमिदम् पूर्नापूर्णमुदच्यते ।
पूर्णस्य पूर्णमादाय पूर्णमेवावशिष्यते ।।
ॐ शान्तिः शान्तिः शान्तिः ।।

Om pūrṇamidaḥ pūrṇamidam pūrṇāpūrṇamudacyate
pūrṇasya pūrṇamādāya pūrṇamevāvaśiṣyate
om śāntiḥ śāntiḥ śāntiḥ

Vocabulary
Om: sound of creation; *pūrṇam-idaḥ*: that is full; *pūrṇam-idam*: this is full; *pūrṇā*: from the full; *pūrṇam-udacyate*: comes the full; *pūrṇam-ādāya*: if the full is taken; *pūrṇasya*: from the full; *pūrṇam-eva*: only the full; *avaśiṣyate*: remains; *om śāntiḥ*: peace of the divine.

Translation
Om, that is full, this is full. From the full comes the full. If the full is taken from the full, only the full remains.

Commentary
The spiritual aspirant invokes this *śānti* mantra before the commencement of the Upaniṣad. All the Upaniṣads begin with an invocation to a god or guru. Here the word 'full' means 'complete' or 'infinite', because only the infinite can be full, having neither beginning nor end. It refers to the unmanifest universe, which is full of divine consciousness, non-dual and unlimited.

First Text

Verses 1 and 2: Brāhmaṇam

।।ब्राह्मणम् १।।

त्रिशिखी ब्राह्मण आदित्यलोकं जगाम तं गत्वोवाच ।

भगवन् किं देहः किं प्राणः किं कारणं किमात्मा ।।१।।

स होवाच सर्वमिदं शिव एव विचानीहि ।

किंतु नित्यः शुद्धो निरञ्जनो विभुरद्वयानन्दः शिव एकः स्वेन भासेदं

सर्वं दृष्ट्वा तप्तायः पिण्डवदेकं भिन्नवदवभासते ।

तद्भ्रासकं किमिति चेदुच्यते ।

सच्छब्दवाच्यमविद्याशबलं ब्रह्म ।।२।।

triśikhī brāhmaṇa ādityalokaṃ jagāma taṃ gatvovāca
bhagavan kiṃ dehaḥ kiṃ prāṇaḥ kiṃ kāraṇaṃ kimātmā (1)
sa hovāca sarvamidaṃ śiva eva vicānīhi kiṃtu nityaḥ
śuddho nirañjano vibhuradvayānandaḥ śiva ekaḥ svena
bhāsedaṃ sarvaṃ dṛṣṭvā taptāyaḥ piṇḍavadekaṃ
bhinnavadavabhāsate
tadbhrāsakaṃ kimiti ceducyate
sacchabdavācyamavidyāśabalaṃ brahma (2)

Vocabulary

brāhmaṇaḥ triśikhī: *brāhmaṇa* with three tufts of hair; *jagāma*: went to; *āditya-lokam*: world of the Sun; *gatvā*: having arrived; *uvāca tam*: he asked Him; *bhagavan*: o Lord; *kim dehaḥ*: what is the body; *kim prāṇaḥ*: what is the breath; *kim kāraṇam*: what is the cause; *kim ātmā*: what is the soul; *sa ha uvāca*: he replied; *sarvam-idam*: all this; *hi*: indeed; *vicā-nī:* leads from the form of; *eva*: only; *śiva*: Śiva; *śiva ekaḥ*: the one Śiva; *nityaḥ*: eternal; *śuddhaḥ*: faultless; *nirañjanaḥ*: pure; *ānandaḥ*: bliss; *vibhu-advaya*: supreme and non-dual; *dṛṣṭvā*: seeing; *sarvam idam*: all this; *svena bhāsa*: with his own light; *avabhāsate*: he shines forth; *ekam bhinnavat*: in different forms;

piṇḍavat: like a mass; *tapta-ayaḥ*: molten iron; *ced-ucyate*: if one asks; *kim-iti*: from where is; *tat-bhrāsakam*: this luminescence; *brahma*: Brahman *śabalam*: replete with; *vidyā*: knowledge; *sat-śabda*: true sound; *vāc-yama*: restraining speech.

Translation

The *brāhmaṇa* with three tufts of hair went to the world of the Sun. Having arrived, he asked Him: "O Lord! What is the body? What is the breath? What is the cause? What is the soul?"

He replied: "All this indeed leads only from the form of Śiva, the one Śiva [who is] eternal, faultless, pure, [whose] bliss [is] supreme and non-dual. Seeing all this with His own light, He shines forth in different forms like a mass [of] molten iron. If one asks from where is this luminescence, [it is] Brahman [who is] replete with the knowledge [of] the true sound [attained through] restraining speech.

Commentary

Here *brāhmaṇa* (or brahmin) refers to a member of the highest caste of traditional Hindu society, a custodian of the revealed wisdom in the Vedas.

A *brāhmaṇaḥ triśikhī* is a brahmin whose head is shaved except for three tufts of hair growing from the top back of the head at the *bindu*, the point between the unmanifest and the manifest, the origin of all sound (*nāda*). *Triśikhī*, three-pronged, refers to the trident of Śiva, and is another name for Śiva.

Āditya refers to the sun as a deity. The Sun is the soul, makes its own fire and light, unaffected by any of the other planets in the solar system, and is therefore creator of all. Thus it is the Sun to whom the brahmin poses the fundamental questions of existence, as, perhaps, he gazes at its solar magnificence as it appears on the horizon. 'He shines forth in different forms' refers to the presence of the light of the Sun in all creation.

Yajnavalkya, an important Upaniṣadic and Brahmanic sage, to whom the *Bṛhadaraṇyaka* is accredited, is said to have received his Vedic mantras directly from the Sun God Āditya. The *Yogi Yajnavalkya* states that 'the Sun, the Self of the world, is the prāṇa placed in the heart'.[1]

'True sound' is the original vibration from which all sound arises. 'Restraining speech' (*vaikhari madhyama*), *mouna* (inner and outer silence), leads us back to knowledge of Brahman, the Absolute, the universal divine power pervading all forms of existence.

Verses 3 and 4: How the World Was Formed

ब्रह्मणोऽव्यक्तम् । अव्यक्तान्महत् । महतोऽहंकारः ।
अहंकारात्पाञ्चतन्मात्राणि । पञ्चतन्मात्रेभ्यः पञ्चमहाभूतानि ।
पञ्चमहाभूतेभ्योऽखिलं जगत् ।।३।।
तदखिलं किमिति । भूतविकारविभागादिरिति ।
एकस्मिन्पिण्डे कथं भूतविकारविभाग इति ।
तत्तत्कार्यकारणभेदरूपेणांशतत्त्ववाचकवाच्यस्थानभेदविषयदेवताकोशभेदविभागा भवन्ति ।।४।।

brahmaṇo 'vyaktam avyaktānmahat mahato 'haṃkāraḥ
ahaṃkārātpañcatanmātrāṇi
pañcatanmātrebhyaḥ pañcamahābhūtāni
pañcamahābhūtebhyo 'khilaṃ jagat (3)
tadakhilaṃ kimiti bhūtavikāravibhāgādiriti
ekasminpiṇḍe kathaṃ bhūtavikāravibhāga iti
tattatkāryakāraṇabhedarūpeṇāṃśatattvavācakavācya-sthānabhedaviṣayadevatākośabhedavibhāgā bhavanti (4)

Vocabulary

brahmaṇaḥ: from Brahman; *avyaktam*: unmanifest; *avyaktāt*: from the unmanifest; *mahat*: greater mind; *mahataḥ*: from the greater mind; *ahaṃkāraḥ*: individual form; *ahaṃkārāt*: from the individual form; *pañca-tanmātrāṇi*: five senses; *pañca-tanmātrebhyaḥ*: from the five senses; *pañca-mahābhūtāni*: five elements; *pañca-mahābhūtebhaḥ*: from the five elements; *akhilam jagat*: entire world; *kim-iti*: what is; *tat-akhilam*: this entire; *ādi*: at the beginning; *vibhāga*: divisions; *vikāra*: changes; *bhūta*: elements; *katham iti*: how was there; *bhūta-vikāra-vibhāga*: divisions and changes in the elements; *ekasmin-piṇḍe*: in each body of matter; *aṃśa-tattva*: parts of the elements; *kārya*: are made; *rūpeṇa*: in the form; *bheda kāraṇa*: different causes; *bhavanti*: they are; *bheda-vibhāgā*: different divisions; *viṣaya*: topics; *devata*: deities; *kośa*:

sheaths; *sthānabheda*: distinction; *vācaka-vācya*: speaker and speech.

Translation

From Brahman [came] the unmanifest; from the unmanifest [came] the greater mind; from the greater mind [came] the individual form; from the individual form [came] the five senses; from the five senses [came] the five elements; from the five elements [came] the entire world.

What is this entire [world]? At the beginning [there were] divisions [and] changes in the elements. How were there divisions and changes in the elements in each body of matter? The parts of the elements are made in the form [of] different causes. They are the different divisions of topics, deities and sheaths, [and] the distinction [between] speaker and speech.

Commentary

Now begins the explanation of how the subtle and material world was formed. Brahman is the cause, and from the cause is the seed of the unmanifest. From the unmanifest comes the greater mind, the universal mind, the pure consciousness pervading the material realm. From the greater mind comes the individual form, ahaṃkāra, literally the 'form of I'. From the individual form come the five senses, sound, touch, sight, taste and smell. From the five senses come the five elements, ether, air, fire, water and earth. All beings in the material world, whether sentient or insentient, are comprised of the same five elemental energies: earth, water, fire, air and ether. Although these five elements are the same in everyone and everything, their proportions are very different, due to a process called *pañcīkaraṇa*, through which the five elements are divided and combined to make the individual forms. Even in our human species, some people are more earthy, while others are more fiery or airy. A further explanation of *pañcīkaraṇa* is in the next section.

Verse 5: Five Elements

अथाकाशोऽन्तःकरणमनोबुद्धिचित्ताहंकाराः ।

वायुः समानोदानव्यानापानप्राणाः ।

वह्निः श्रोत्रत्वक्चक्षुर्जिह्वाघ्राणानि ।

आपः शब्दस्पर्शरूपरसगन्धाः ।

पृथिवी वाक्पाणिपादपायूपस्थाः ।।५।।

athākāśo'ntaḥkaraṇamanobuddhicittāhaṃkārāḥ
vāyuḥ samānodānavyānāpānaprāṇāḥ
vahniḥ śrotratvakcakṣurjihvāghrāṇāni
āpaḥ śabdasparśarūparasagandhāḥ
pṛthivī vākpāṇipādapāyūpasthāḥ (5)

Vocabulary

atha: now; *ākāśaḥ*: ether; *antaḥ karaṇa*: instrument of the mind; *manas*: thinking mind; *buddhi*: discerning mind; *citta*: memory, individual consciousness; *ahaṃkāra*: individual self; *vāyuḥ*: air; *samāna*: sideways moving energy between navel and diaphragm; *udāna*: energy moving in arms, legs and head; *vyāna*: energy pervading whole body; *apāna*: downward moving energy from navel; *prāṇa*: vital energy; upward moving energy in thoracic area; *vahniḥ*: fire; *śrotra*: ears; *tvak*: skin; *cakṣuḥ*: eyes; *jihvā*: tongue; *āghrāṇa*: nose; *āpaḥ*: water; *śabda*: sound; *sparśa*: touch; *rūpa*: appearance; *rasa*: taste; *gandha*: smell; *pṛthivī*: earth; *vāk*: speech; *pāṇi*: hands; *pāda*: feet; *pāyu*: anus; *upastha*: genital organs.

Translation

Now ether [includes] the *antaḥ karaṇa*, *manas*, *buddhi*, *citta* and *ahaṃkāra*. Air [includes] *samāna*, *udāna*, *vyāna, apāna* and *prāṇa.* Fire [includes] ears, skin, eyes, tongue and nose. Water [includes] sound, touch, appearance, taste and smell. Earth [includes] speech, hands, feet, anus and genital organs.

Commentary

The word *ākāśa* signifies that which provides space for

solid forms to exist. It comes from the verb *kāś*, to shine or appear. Ākāśa tattwa, the ether element, is responsible for all perception of sound, be it gross, subtle or causal, transmitted through the sense organ '*śrotra*' ear. In the body it controls space around the organs. In the mind it governs emotions and desires. Ether, the most subtle element, includes *antaḥ karaṇa*, 'inner instrument', which is comprised of four organs: *manas*, the rational thinking mind which deals with information received from the senses; *buddhi*, higher mind or wisdom; *citta*, storehouse of memories; and *ahaṃkāra*, ego or identification with the lower individual self. Through the antaḥ karaṇa and its four organs flows pure consciousness, which is not easy to realise, as all four organs are influenced by the three *guṇas, sattwa, rajas* and *tamas*.

The air element is mobility in all directions. In the body it is respiration and the conversion of air to energy and movement of the five prāṇas, viz. physical *prāṇa*, movement in the area of the heart and lungs; *samāna*: sideways moving energy between navel and diaphragm; *udāna*: energy moving in arms, legs and head; *vyāna*: energy pervading whole body; and *apāna*: downward moving energy from navel.

Agni, the fire element, contains all the sense organs (*indriyas*), including antaḥ karaṇa, because fire is responsible for vitality and stimulation. The fire element heats, stimulates, burns and transforms. In the body it is the digestive system and metabolism. The water element represents the force of attraction, enabling flow, circulation, rhythm, fluidity and fluid movement. In the mind it is the steady flow of thoughts from one idea to another, creating thoughts and emotions regarding self-gratification. The earth element represents stability. It is the pull of gravity and force which binds things together. Physically, it is the skeletal system, blood vessels, connective tissue and that which binds each cell together.

Verse 6: Functions of the Elements

ज्ञानसंकल्पनिश्चयानुसंधानाभिमाना आकाशकार्यान्तःकरणविषयाः ।
समीकरणोन्नयनग्रहणश्रवणोच्छ्वासा वायुकार्यप्राणादिविषयाः ।
शब्दस्पर्शरूपरसगान्धा अग्निकार्यज्ञानेन्द्रियविषया अबाश्रिताः ।
वानादानगमनविसर्गानन्दाः पृथिवीकार्यकर्मेन्द्रिय विषयाः ।
कर्मज्ञानेन्द्रियविषयेषु प्राणतन्मात्रविषया अन्तर्भूतः ।
मनोबुद्ध्योश्चित्ताहंकारौ चान्तर्भूतौ ।।६।।

jñānasaṃkalpaniścayānusaṃdhānābhimānā ākāśakāryāntaḥkaraṇaviṣayāḥ samīkaraṇonnayanagrahaṇaśravaṇocdhvāsā vāyukāryaprāṇādiviṣayāḥ śabdasparśarūparasagandhā agnikāryajñānendriyaviṣayā abāśritaḥ vacanādānagamanavisargānandāḥ pṛthivīkāryakarmendriya viṣayāḥ karmajñānendriyaviṣayeṣu prāṇatanmātraviṣayā antarbhūtaḥ manobuddhyościttāhaṃkārau cāntarbhūtau (6)

Vocabulary

jñāna: knowledge; *saṃkalpa*: purpose; *niścaya*: determination; *anusaṃdhāna*: inquiry; *abhimānā*: desire; *ākāśa-kārya*: functions [of] the ether element; *antaḥkaraṇa-viṣayāḥ*: scope of the mind; *samīkaraṇa*: uniting; *unnayana*: elevating; *grahaṇa*: holding; *śravaṇa*: hearing; *uddhvāsā*: exhaling; *vāyu-kārya*: functions of the air element; *prāṇa-ādi-viṣayāḥ*: scope of the *prāṇas*; *śabda*: sound; *sparśa*: touch; *rūpa*: appearance; *rasa*: taste; *gandha*: smell; *agni-kārya*: functions of the fire element; *jñānendriya-viṣayā*: scope of the organs of perception; *āśritaḥ*: they are related to; *ap*: element of water; *vacana*: speech; *ādāna*: receiving; *gamana*: moving; *visarga*: voiding; *ānanda*: pleasure; *pṛthivī-kārya*: functions of the earth element; *karmendriya viṣayāḥ*: scope of the organs of action; *prāṇa-tanmātra-viṣayā*: domains of *prāṇa* and *tanmātra*; *antarbhūtaḥ*: are contained; *karma- jñāna-indriya-viṣayeṣu*: in the domains of the organs of perception and action; *ca*: and; *citta-ahaṃkārau*: memory and individual sense; *antarbhūtau*: are both contained in; *manaḥ-buddhyoḥ*: thinking and discerning mind.

Translation

Knowledge, purpose, determination, inquiry [and] desire [are in] the scope of the mind [and] functions of the ether element. Uniting, elevating, holding, hearing [and] exhaling [are] in the scope of the *prāṇas* [and] functions of the air element. Sound, touch, appearance, taste [and] smell [are] in the scope of the organs of perception [and] functions of the fire element. They are related to the element of water. Speech, receiving, moving, voiding [and] pleasure [are] in the scope of the organs of action [and] functions of the earth element.

The domains of *prāṇa* and *tanmātra* are contained in the domains of [both] the organs of perception and action. Citta and ahaṃkāra are both contained in manas and buddhi.

Commentary

Each element covers a range of characteristics and activities which are expressed through a particular sense organ and organ of action, as described above. The five elements are also known as the manifest or *vyakta tattwas*, meaning that they perform a specific job.

The prāṇas and tanmātras are expressed through both the sense organs and the organs of action. 'The sense organs represent constant and ceaseless activity of the elements in the body'[2], whether awake or asleep. Prāṇa even continues to flow for some time after death. Citta and ahaṃkāra are both interwoven with manas and buddhi.

Verse 7: Tanmātra

अवकाशविधूतदर्शनपिण्डीकरणधारणाः सूक्ष्मतमा जैवतन्मात्रविषयाः ।।७।।

avakāśavidhūtadarśanapiṇḍīkaraṇadhāraṇāḥ sūkṣmatamā jaivatanmātraviṣayāḥ (7)

Vocabulary

sūkṣmatamāḥ viṣayāḥ: most subtle parts; *jaiva-tanmātra*: personal *tanmātras*; *avakāśa*: space; *vidhūta*: spreading; *darśana*: seeing; *piṇḍīkaraṇa*: combining; *dhāraṇā*: stability.

Translation

The most subtle parts [of] the personal tanmātras [are] space, spreading, seeing, combining [and] stability.

Commentary

Swami Satyasangananda, in her book *Tattwa Shuddhi*, defines *tanmātra* as the 'subtle or primary essence of *gandha* (smell), *rasa* (taste), *rūpa* (sight or form), *sparśa* (touch) and *śabda* (sound), from which the grosser elements or *tattwas* are produced'.[3] Swami Niranjananda, in his book *Yoga Darshan*, says *tanmātra* means 'the nature or quality of the elements'. The nature of fire, he says, is 'to burn, to radiate heat, to provide warmth and light'.[4]

The personal *tanmātras* are those expressed in each body. So 'space' refers to the space of the mind in the ether, 'spreading' to the circulation of prāṇa in the air element, 'seeing' to sight given by the fire element, 'combining' to the fluidity of the water element, and 'stability' to the solid body supported by bones and organs in the earth element. In kundalini yoga, the tattwas and the tanmātras relate to the cakras. So the element of *mūlādhāra* is earth, and its tanmātra is smell.

Verse 8: Deities of the Twelve Nāḍīs

एवं द्वादशाङ्गानि आध्यात्मिकान्याधिभौतिकान्याधिदैविकानि ।

अत्र निशाकरचतुर्मुखदिग्वातार्कवरुणाश्व्यग्नीन्द्रेपेन्द्रप्रजापतियमा

इत्यक्षाधिदेवतारूपैर्द्वादशनाड्यन्तःप्रवृत्ताः प्राणा एवाङ्गानि

अंगज्ञानं तदेव ज्ञातेति ।।८।।

तद्योगं च द्विधा विद्धि पूर्वोत्तरविधानतः ।

पूर्वं तु तारकं विद्यादमनस्कं तदुत्तरमिति ।।८।।

evaṃ dvādaśāṅgāni ādhyātmikānyādhibhautikānyādhi daivikāni atra niśākaracaturmukhadigvātārkavaruṇāś - vyagnīndrependraprajāpatiyamā ityakṣādhidevatārūpairdvādaśanāḍyantaḥpravṛttāḥ prāṇā evāṅgāni aṃgajñānaṃ tadeva jñāteti (8)

Vocabulary

evam: thus; *dvādaśa-aṅgāni*: twelve parts; *anya*: those; *ādhi*: relating to; *ādhyātmika*: spiritual Self; *bhautika*: physical; *daivikāni*: Divine; *atra*: here; *iti*: it is said; *niśākara*: moon; *caturmukha*: four-faced one; *dik*: directions; *vāta*: wind; *arka*: sun; *varuṇa*: ocean; *aśvī*: Aśvini; *pravṛttāḥ*: move as; *prāṇā aṅgāni*: components of *prāṇa*; *dvādaśa-nāḍyantaḥ*: twelve *nāḍīs*; *rūpaiḥ*: in the forms; *adhidevatā*: presiding deities; *akṣa*: senses; *iti*: it is said; *jñātā tat*: knows this; *aṃga-jñānam*: knowledge of the Self.

Translation

Thus, the twelve parts [include] those which relate to the spiritual Self, the physical [and] the Divine. Here, it is said, the moon, the four-faced one, the directions, wind, sun, ocean, Aśvini, Agni, Indra, Upendra, Prajāpati [and] Yama move as components of *prāṇa* in the twelve *nāḍīs* in the forms [of] presiding deities [of] the senses. It is said [that whoever] knows this [has] knowledge of the Self.

Commentary

This text says there are twelve main *nāḍīs*, whereas *Yoga Cudāmani Upaniṣad* says there are ten, and *Śāṇḍilya Upaniṣad, Gheranda Saṃhita, Hatha Yoga Pradipika* and *Yoga Sūtras* describe fourteen major nāḍīs. As there are 72,000 nāḍīs in the body, the the number of major ones depends on how the psychic body is perceived by the individual.

Agni, Vāyu and Soma are the great Vedic deities of Fire, Air and Moon. Agni, the deity of earth, has the qualities of fire and willpower, and is the fire of the *kuṇḍalinī*. Vāyu, the diety of air, is responsible for prāṇa, prāṇāyama and wind. Soma, the deity of the moon, the cosmic waters, relates to the higher mind. Sūrya (*arka*) is light, the light of pure consciousness.[5] Lord Brahma, the Creator, is often depicted as having four faces, which symbolise the four Vedas and the four directions.

There are eight deities (*aṣṭa dikpāla* 'eight guardians of a quarter of the sky') which govern the eight directions. They are Kubera (North), Yama (South), Indra (East), Varuṇa (West), Isana (North East), Agni (South East), Vāyu (North West), Nirrti (South West).

The sense organ of the ears has the deity of directions presiding over it. The deity of air presides over the function of the skin. The sun is the deity for eyes. The water god, Varuna, is the deity of the sense of taste and the beautiful divine physicians, Ashwini twins, preside over the sense of smell. Sūrya, the sun god, is the father of the Aśvinī twins, depicted as divine doctors, who ride in a horse-drawn (*aśva* horse) golden chariot bringing healing energy and rejuvenation to earth-bound beings. Upendra, a younger brother of Indra, is another name of Viṣṇu, preserver of the universe. Prajāpati, literally 'lord of created beings', is another name of Brahma, the creator. Yama, 'restrainer', is the deity of death, the south direction and the underworld.

Verse 9: Synthesis of the Five Elements

अथ व्योमानिलानलजलपृथिव्योनानां पञ्चीकरणमिति ।
ज्ञातृत्वं समानयोगेन श्रोत्रद्वारा शब्दगुणो
वागधिष्ठित आकाशे तिष्ठति आकाशस्तिष्ठति ।
मनो व्यानयोगेन त्वग्द्वारा स्पर्शगुणः पाण्यधिष्ठितो
वायौ तिष्ठति वायुस्तिष्ठति ।
बुद्धिरुदानयोगेन चक्षुर्द्वारा रूपगुणः पादाधिष्ठितोऽग्नौ
तिष्ठत्यग्निस्तिष्ठति ।
चित्तमपानयोगेन जिह्वाद्वारा रसगुण उपस्थाधिष्ठितोऽप्सु
तिष्ठत्यापस्तिष्ठन्ति ।
अहंकारः प्राणयोगेन घ्राणद्वारा गन्धगुणो गुदाधिष्ठितः
पृथिव्यां तिष्ठति पृथिवी तिष्ठति य एवं वेद ।।९।।

atha vyomānilānalajalapṛthivyonānāṃ pañcīkaraṇamiti
jñātṛtvaṃ samānayogena śrotradvārā śabdaguṇo
vāgadhiṣṭhita ākāśe tiṣṭhati ākāśastiṣṭhati
mano vyānayogena tvagdvārā sparśaguṇaḥ pāṇyadhiṣṭhito
vāyau tiṣṭhati vāyustiṣṭhati
buddhirudānayogena cakṣurdvārā rūpaguṇaḥ
pādādhiṣṭhito'gnau tiṣṭhatyagnistiṣṭhati
cittamapānayogena jihvādvārā rasaguṇa
upasthādhiṣṭhito'psu tiṣṭhatyāpastiṣṭhanti
ahaṃkāraḥ prāṇayogena ghrāṇadvārā gandhaguṇo
gudādhiṣṭhitaḥ
pṛthivyāṃ tiṣṭhati pṛthivī tiṣṭhati ya evaṃ veda (9)

Vocabulary

atha: now; *pañcīkaraṇam*: synthesis of the five elements; *nānām*: different *vyomā-anila-anala-jala-pṛthivāḥ*: ether, wind, fire, water, earth; *iti*: is explained; *tiṣṭhati ākāśaḥ*: here is ether; *jñātṛtva*: inner knowledge; *samāna-yogena*: together with samāna; *śabda-guṇaḥ*: quality of sound; *śrotra-dvārā*: through the ear; *vāk-adhiṣṭhitaḥ*: regulated by the vocal cords;

tiṣṭhati ākāśe: abides in the ether; *tiṣṭhati vāyu*: here is air; *manaḥ*: thinking mind; *vyāna-yogena*: together with vyāna; *sparśa-guṇaḥ*: quality of touch; *tvag-dvārā*: through the skin; *pāṇi-adhiṣṭhitaḥ*: connected with the hands; *tiṣṭhati vāyuḥ*: abides in the air; *tiṣṭhati agniḥ*: here is fire; *buddhiḥ*: discerning mind; *udāna-yogena*: together with udāna; *rūpa-guṇaḥ*: quality of sight; *cakṣuḥ-dvārā*: through the eyes; *pāda-adhiṣṭhitaḥ*: dependent on the feet; *tiṣṭhati agnau*: abides in the fire; *āpaḥ-tiṣṭhanti*: here is water; *cittam*: memory; *apāna-yogena*: together with apāna; *rasa-guṇaḥ*: quality of taste; *jihvādvārā*: through the tongue; *upastha-adhiṣṭhitaḥ*: connected with the genitals; *tiṣṭhati apsu*: abides in water; *tiṣṭhati pṛthivī*: earth; *ahaṃkāraḥ*: individual self; *prāṇa-yogena*: together with prāṇa; *gandha-guṇaḥ*: quality of smell; *ghrāṇa-dvārā*: through the nose; *guda-adhiṣṭhitaḥ*: connected with the anus; *tiṣṭhati pṛthivyām*: abides in water; *yaḥ veda*: whoever knows; *evam*: thus.

Translation

Now the synthesis of the five different elements, ether, wind, fire, water and earth, is explained. Here is [the element of] ether: inner knowledge together with samāna, [having] the quality of sound [which comes] through the ear [and] is regulated by the vocal cords, abides in the ether. Here is [the element of] air: the mind together with vyāna, [having] the quality of touch through the skin [and] connected with the hands, abides in the air. Here is [the element of] fire: the discerning mind together with udāna, [having] the quality of sight through the eyes [and] dependent on the feet, abides in the fire. Here is [the element of] water: memory together with apāna, [having] the quality of taste through the tongue [and] connected with the genitals, abides in water. Here is [the element of] earth: the individual self together with prāṇa, [having] the quality of smell through the nose, connected with the anus, abides in earth. Whoever knows thus [is a yogin].

Commentary
This verse lists some of the characteristics of each element, viz. the state of mind, the sub-prāṇa (*prāṇa vāyu*), the sense (tanmātra), sense organ and the organ of action.

Tattwa Shuddhi differs from this verse in the locations of the sub-prāṇas. It states that vyāna moves in ether, udāna moves in air, samāna moves in fire, prāṇa moves in water and apāna moves in earth.[6]

The tattwas are not physical or chemical elements. They are creations of vibrations of energy or prāṇa, which pervade the whole body and mind. All our actions and thoughts are constantly influenced by them. Therefore the yogin must have a complete understanding of the tattwas, their functions and influences, so that they can be well managed.

मन्त्र २

Second Text

अत्रैते श्लोका भवन्ति ।।

atraite ślokā bhavanti

Translation

The [relevant] *ślokas* are here [below].

Verses 1 to 4a: Division and Combination of the Elements

पृथग्भूते षोडश कलाः स्वार्धभागान्परान्क्रमात् ।
अन्तःकरणव्यानाक्षिरसपायुनभः क्रमात् ।।१।।
मुख्यात्पूर्वोत्तरैर्भूतेभूते चतुश्चतुः ।
पूर्वमाकाशमाश्रित्य पृथिव्यादिषु संस्थिताः ।।२।।
एवंशो ह्यभूतस्मात्तेभ्यश्चांशो ह्यभूत्तथा ।।३।।
तस्मादन्योन्यमाश्रित्य ह्योतं प्रोतमनुक्रमात् ।४।

pṛthagbhūte ṣoḍaśa kalāḥ svārdhabhāgānparānkramāt
antaḥkaraṇavyānākṣirasapāyunabhaḥ kramāt (1)
mukhyātpūrvottarairbhūtebhūte catuścatuḥ
pūrvamākāśamāśritya pṛthivyādiṣu saṃsthitāḥ (2)
evaṃśo hyabhūttasmāttebhyaścāṃśo hyabhūttathā (3)
tasmādanyonyamāśritya hyotaṃ protamanukramāt (4a)

Vocabulary

pṛthak-bhūte: in [each] separate element; *ṣoḍaśa kalāḥ*: sixteen parts; *kramāt*: by degrees; *ardha-parān-bhāgān*: two equal parts; *antaḥkaraṇa-vyāna-akṣi-rasa-pāyu-nabhaḥ*: mind, wind, eyes, essence, anus [and] nose; *mukhyāt*: first and foremost; *bhūte-bhūte*: in each element; *pūrvottaraiḥ*: preceding and following; *catuḥ*: four; *pūrvam āśritya*: starting with; *ākāśam*: ether; *saṃsthitāḥ*: concluding; *pṛthivī-ādiṣu*: with earth and the others;*tasmāt eva*: that is why; *aṃśaḥ*: section; *bhūt*: made; *tebhyaḥ*: from them; *tathā*: in that way;

āśritya: dependent on; *anyonyam*: one another; *protam*: is fixed; *tasmāt anukramāt*: by this method.

Translation

In [each] separate element the sixteen parts [are formed] by degrees [into] two equal parts, [and] by degrees [into] mind, wind, eyes, essence, anus [and] nose. First and foremost, in each element, preceding and following, [there are] four [parts], [then] four [again], starting with ether [and] concluding with earth and the others. That is why [each] section [that is] made from them, [the other] sections are made in that way. Dependent on one another, [each] is fixed by this method.

Commentary

The five elements (*pañca tattwa* or *pañcabhūta*) of nature are divided and combined to form gross individual matter. For example, one half of the ether element combines with one eighth of each of the air, fire, water and earth elements. One half of the air combines with one eighth of each of the ether, fire, water and earth elements, etc. This process is called quintuplication. After this, different permutations and combinations are formed. This process of converting subtle elements into gross matter is called *pañcikāraṇa*, and is responsible for all physical matter. The ratio of the elements in the human body is said to be 5:4:3:2:1 from earth to ether. Only Nature knows the exact combinations and permutations of physical matter. [7]

The *Chandogya Upanishad* teaches the doctrine of *Trivṛtkāraṇa*, from which developed the *Vedantic Theory of Pañcikāraṇa*. Later Ādi Śaṅkarācārya wrote the treatise *Pañcikāraṇam*, which was expounded by his disciple Sureśvarācārya.

Verses 4b and 5: What the World Consists Of

पञ्चभूतमयी भूमिः सा चेतनसमन्विता ॥४॥

तत ओषधयोऽन्नं च ततः पिण्डाश्चतुर्विधाः ।

रसासृङ्मांसमेदोऽस्थिमज्जाशुक्राणि धातवः ॥५॥

pañcabhūtamayī bhūmiḥ sā cetanasamanvitā (4b)
tata oṣadhayo'nnaṃ ca tataḥ piṇḍāścaturvidhāḥ
rasāsṛṅmāṃsamedo'sthimajjāśukrāṇi dhātavaḥ (5)

Vocabulary

bhūmiḥ: world; *pañca-bhūta-mayī*: consisting of the five elements; *samanvitā*: possesses; *cetana*: consciousness; *annam*: food; *dhayaḥ*: possessing; *oṣa*: medicine; *ca tataḥ*: and then; *catuḥ-vidhāḥ*: four kinds; *piṇḍāḥ*: forms; *dhātavaḥ*: constituents; *rasa-asṛṅ-māṃsa-medaḥ-asthimajjā-śukrāṇi*: fluid, blood, flesh, fat, bone, marrow [and] sexual fluid.

Translation

The world, consisting of the five elements possesses consciousness, food possessing medicine, and then four kinds [of] forms, [and] the constituents [of] fluid, blood, flesh, fat, bone, marrow [and] sexual fluid.

Commentary

Consciousness, from which everything arises, pervades the five elements of nature, producing plants which both nourish and heal. Plants have specific needs: light (fire), air, water, nutrients (from the earth) and space. All living things need space, air, water and food, which comes from plants and also animals who eat plants.

The seven constituents (*dhātus*) are the evolutes of the five elements, and are the fundamental tissue layers of the body responsible for its formation, support and survival.

All earthly beings are influenced by the dhātus, which give substance and structure to the tissues, organs and systems of the body. They are *rasa*, lymph or fluid; *rakta*, blood; *mansa*, muscle; *meda*, fat and hormones; *asthi*, bone and connective tissue; *majja*, bone marrow and nerves; and *śukra*, reproductive fluid.

Consciousness permeates the seven constituents (*dhātus*) of the individual body. Fluids (*rasa*, literally 'sap' or 'juice') are tissue fluids, including chyle, lymph and blood plasma, as well as breast milk and menstrual blood. Blood refers to the red blood cells, blood vessels and tendons. Flesh is skeletal muscle, ligaments and skin. Fat is fat in the limbs and torso. Bone includes all bones and teeth. Marrow is that which is inside a bone: red and yellow bone marrow, the brain and spinal cord. Sexual fluid includes both male and female sexual fluids.

Each of these seven constituents has a particular function. The function of fluids is nourishment. The function of blood is invigoration. The function of flesh is to plaster the skeleton. Lubrication is the function of fat. Bones support the body. Marrow fills up the bones. The purpose of sexual fluids is reproduction, and the production of *ojas*, which controls immunity and generates the aura, the subtle energy field within and around the body.

There are waste products from each constituent. The waste product of fluids is mucus, of blood is bile, of fat is sweat, of marrow is tears. The wastes of flesh accumulate in the cavities of the body, such as ear wax, nasal mucus and navel lint. The wastes of bones are all body hair and nails. [8]

Verses 6 to 8: Forms of the Elements

केचित्तद्योगतः पिण्डा भूतेभ्यः संभवाः क्वचित् ।
तस्मिनन्नमयः पिण्डो नाभिमण्डलसंस्थितः ।।६।।
अस्य मध्येऽस्ति हृदयं सनालं पद्मकोशवत् ।
सत्त्वानतर्वार्तिनो देवाः कर्त्रहंकारचेतनाः ।।७।।
अस्य बीजं तमःपिण्डं मोहरूपं जडं घनम् ।
वर्तते कण्ठमाश्रित्य मिश्रीभूतमिदं जगत् ।।८।।

kecittadyogataḥ piṇḍā bhūtebhyaḥ saṃbhavāḥ kvacit
tasminannamayaḥ piṇḍo nābhimaṇḍalasaṃsthitaḥ (6)
asya madhye'sti hṛdayaṃ sanālaṃ padmakośavat
sattvāntarvārtino devāḥ kartrahaṃkāracetanāḥ (7)
asya bījaṃ tamaḥpiṇḍaṃ moharūpaṃ jaḍaṃ ghanam
vartate kaṇṭhamāśritya miśrībhūtamidaṃ jagat (8)

Vocabulary

tat-cit-yogataḥ: this apparent combination; *kvacit*: then; *saṃbhavāḥ*: possibilities; *piṇḍāḥ*: crystals; *bhūtebhyaḥ*: from the elements; *piṇḍaḥ*: form; *anna-mayaḥ*: made of food; *saṃsthitaḥ*: remains; *tasmin*: here; *nābhi-maṇḍala*: region of the navel; *hṛdayam*: heart; *asti*: has; *sanālam*: stalk; *padma-kośa-vat*: like the calyx of a lotus; *asya madhye*: in its middle; *devāḥ*: gods; *cetanāḥ*: whose consciousness; *kartṛ*: destroyer; *ahaṃkāra*: ego; *sattva-antarvārtināḥ*: dwell in harmony; *asya bījam*: its seed; *vartate*: exists; *kaṇṭham*: throat; *tamaḥ-piṇḍam*: in the form of *tamas*; *moha-rūpam*: consisting of delusion; *ghanam*: mass; *jaḍam*: ignorance; *āśritya*: dependent on; *idam jagat*: this world; *miśrī-bhūtam*: mixed elements.

Translation

[Because of] this apparent combination [of elements], [there are] then possibilities [of] crystals [made] from the elements. The form made of food remains here in the region of the navel.

The heart has a stalk like the calyx of a lotus in its middle, [and] the gods whose consciousness [is] the destroyer [of] the ego dwell in harmony [there]. Its seed exists [in] the throat as 'material particles of potential energy'[9] consisting of delusion [and] a mass [of] ignorance, dependent on this world of mixed elements.

Commentary

When parts of the subtle elements combine with each other, they crystallise, that is form as particles of matter. The matter which is food goes to the stomach. Through the heart centre, *anāhata cakra*, rises *suṣumnā nāḍī*, which is like the stalk of a lotus. Here one begins to transcend the limited ego and experience peace. At the centre of the anāhata cakra is the *bīja mantra yam* यं, and within its *bindu* are the all-pervasive deity Īśa, who is as radiant as the sun, and the auspicious goddess Kakinī, who is four-armed having the knowledge of the four directions, yellow like the sun, and who sees the inner and outer life with her three eyes.

The seed the verse refers to is *bindu visarga* from which the nectar drips down to *viśuddhi cakra* at the throat. Bindu produces nectar when both bindu and viśuddhi are stimulated, and poison when viśuddhi is not stimulated. In this verse the poison is ignorance and delusion.

Verse 9: Ātman at Sahasrāra

प्रत्यगानन्दरूपात्मा मूर्ध्नि स्थाने परे पदे ।
अनन्तशक्तिसंयुक्तो जगद्रूपेण भासते ॥९॥

pratyagānandarūpātmā mūrdhni sthāne pare
pade anantaśaktisaṃyukto jagadrūpeṇa bhāsate

Vocabulary

rūpa: form; *pratyak-ānanda*: Supreme Bliss; *ātmā*: *ātman*, Supreme Consciousness; *sthāne*: situated; *mūrdhni*: crown of the head; *saṃyuktaḥ*: endowed with; *ananta-śakti*: infinite *śakti*; *bhāsate*: it shines; *pare pade*: in the highest position; *jagat-rūpeṇa*: through its worldly form.

Translation

The *ātman* [is] the form of Supreme Bliss situated at the crown [of] the head. Endowed with the infinite *śakti*, it shines in the highest position through its worldly form.

Commentary

The *ātman* is the permanent Self which pervades the mind and body, yet transcends mind, body, space and time. According to the *Mandukya Upaniṣad* it is pure awareness, peace, bliss and non-duality.[10] The crown of the head refers to *sahasrāra*, symbolised by the thousand-petalled lotus, where awareness is infinitely expanded beyond the limited self. Sahasrāra is sometimes called the seventh cakra, but it is not a cakra. It is the container of *śakti*, primal power and potential. The six lower cakras, from *mūlādhāra* to *ājñā*, are switches which activate the pervasive power of sahasrāra within them.

Just as the sun's light shines on all beings, so the light of the *paramātman*, the Supreme Soul, radiates throughout the whole world.

Verses 10 and 11: Four States of Consciousness

सर्वत्र वर्तते जाग्रत्स्वप्नं जाग्रति वर्तते ।
सुषुप्तं च तुरीयं च नान्यावस्थासु कुत्रचित् ॥१०॥
सर्वदेशेष्वनुस्यूतश्चतूरूपः शिवात्मकः ।
यथा महाफले सर्वे रसाः सर्वप्रवर्तकाः ॥११॥

sarvatra vartate jāgratsvapnaṃ jāgrati vartate
suṣuptaṃ ca turīyaṃ ca nānyāvasthāsu kutracit (10)
sarvadeśeṣvanusyūtaścatūrūpaḥ śivātmakaḥ
yathā mahāphale sarve rasāḥ sarvapravartakāḥ (11)

Vocabulary

jāgrat: waking; *vartate*: is; *sarvatra*: everywhere; *svapnam*: dreaming; *jāgrati*: in waking; *suṣuptam*: deep sleep; *ca*: and; *turīyam*: state beyond; *na kutracit*: nowhere; *anya-avasthāsu*: in the other states; *yathā*: just as; *rasāḥ*: tastes; *pravartakāḥ*: are produced; *sarve mahā-phale*: in every great fruit; *catūrūpaḥ*: four states; *śiva-ātmakaḥ*: pervaded by the essence of Śiva; *anusyūtaḥ*: are strung together; *sarva-deśeṣu*: in all the states.

Translation

The waking [state] is everywhere. Dreaming is in the waking [state]. Deep sleep and the state beyond are nowhere in the other states. Just as tastes are produced in every great fruit, [so] the four states pervaded by the essence of Śiva are strung together in all the states.

Commentary

The waking state is the state of consciousness related to the senses and the material world. It is the first state of consciousness, and is everywhere coming from prāṇa. The senses are externalised. It is related to 'A', the first sound of Aum, according to the *Mandukya Upaniṣad*.

From waking comes dreaming, the subconscious realm of the mind, the 'U' of Aum. In deep sleep the senses are withdrawn both from the external world and the contents of the mind, the 'M' of Aum. Although *turīya*, the fourth state, is the state beyond the states of waking, dreaming and sleeping, the cosmic pure consciousness which is the essence of Śiva, pervades all four states.

Verses 12 and 13: Koṣa

तथैवान्नमये कोशे कोशास्तिष्ठन्ति जान्तरे ।

यथा कोशस्तथा जीवो यथा जीवस्तथा शिवः ॥१२॥

सविकारस्तथा जीवो निर्विकारस्तथा शिवः ।

कोशास्तस्य विकारास्ते ह्यवस्थासु प्रवर्तकाः ॥१३॥

tathaivānnamaye kośe kośāstiṣṭhanti jāntare yathā kośastathā jīvo yathā jīvastathā śivaḥ (12)
savikārastathā jīvo nirvikārastathā śivaḥ kośāstasya vikārāste hyavasthāsu pravartakāḥ (13)

Vocabulary

tathaiva: likewise; *kośāḥ tiṣṭhanti ja*: sheaths are produced; *antare annamaye kośe*: within *annamaya kośa*; *yathā kośaḥ*: just as the kośa; *jīvaḥ*: individual soul; *tathā jīvaḥ śivaḥ*: so the individual soul [is] Śiva; *tathā*: thus; *jīvaḥ savikāraḥ*: individual [is] changeable; *śivaḥ nirvikāraḥ*: Śiva [is] unchangeable; *kośāḥ tasya vikārāḥ*: kośas have differences; *pravartakāḥ*: are produced; *avasthāsu*: states of existence.

NB: in these verses the word for 'sheath' is spelt kośa. The usual spelling is koṣa, which I have used below.

Translation

Likewise, *koṣas* are produced within *annamaya koṣa*, just as the koṣa is the individual soul, so the individual soul [is] Śiva. Thus, the individual [is] changeable, [but] Śiva [is] unchangeable. The koṣas have differences which are produced in the states of existence.

Commentary

Koṣas are defined as sheaths, layers and bodies: sheaths because they are a covering, an envelope or a coating; layers because they are like sheets or covers; and bodies because they contain energies of the five elements.

They are *annamaya koṣa*, the solid physical body; *prāṇamaya koṣa*, the vital or pranic body; *manomaya koṣa*, the mental body; *vijñānamaya koṣa*, the body of intuition and spiritual knowledge; and *ānandamaya* koṣa, the body of pure spiritual bliss. These last four sheaths interact within the physical body. The five sheaths co-exist with their differences in the individual, yet are permeated by pure unchangeable consciousness.

Verses 14 and 15: Renunciation

यथा रसाशये फेनं मथनादेव जायते ।

मनोनिर्मथनादेव विकल्पा बहवस्तथा ॥१४॥

कर्मणा वर्तते कर्मो तत्त्यागाच्छान्तिमाप्नुयात् ।

अयने दक्षिणे प्राप्ते प्रपञ्चाभिमुखं गतः ॥१५॥

yathā rasāśaye phenaṃ mathanādeva jāyate
manonirmathanādeva vikalpā bahavastathā (14)
karmaṇā vartate karmo tattyāgācchāntimāpnuyāt
ayane dakṣiṇe prāpte prapañcābhimukhaṃ gataḥ (15)

Vocabulary
yathā: just as; *phenam*: foam; *jāyate*: is produced; *mathanāt*: by churning; *rasa*: liquid; *āśaye*: in a receptacle; *tathā*: similarly; *nirmathanāt*: by churning; *manaḥ*: mind; *bahavaḥ vikalpāḥ*: many false notions; *karmaṇā*: through action; *karmaḥ vartate*: *karma* exists; *tyāgāt*: through renunciation; *āpnuyāt*: one obtains; *śāntim*: peace; *prāpte*: if one arrives; *dakṣine ayane*: by the southern way; *gataḥ abhimukham*: one faces; *prapañca*: visible world.

Translation
Just as foam is produced by churning liquid in a receptacle, similarly by churning the mind many false notions [arise]. Through action karma exists. Through renunciation one obtains peace. If one arrives by the southern way, one faces the visible world.

Commentary
Yogaḥ-citta-vṛtti-nirodhaḥ: this well-known definition of yoga in the Yoga-Sūtra of Patañjali is translated by Georg Feuerstein as 'yoga is the restriction of fluctuations of consciousness', [11] consciousness here referring to all thoughts, memories etc which float on the surface of the mind, preventing awareness of the inner depths of the mind.

The many false notions refer to the five causes of affliction (*kleśa*): ignorance (*avidyā*), ego (*asmita* lit. I-am-ness), attraction (*rāga*), aversion (*dveṣa*) and fear of death (*abhiniveṣa*). The first one, ignorance, gives rise to the other four.

Through these causes action arises. Through action comes karma, the results of the action. One who no longer identifies with the results of one's actions reaches a state of deep peace.

Dakṣiṇāyana, the southern way, is called thus, because here the sun appears to move on its course towards the south. This path leads to rebirth on earth, darkness and further association with the ancestors and relations. [12]

Verse 16 to 18: Satsang

अहंकाराभिमानेन जीवः स्याद्धि सदाशिवः ।

स चाविवेकप्रकृतिसङ्गत्या तत्र मुह्यते ।।१६।।

नानायोनिशतं गत्वा शेतेऽसौ वासनावशात् ।

विमोक्षात्संचरत्येव मत्स्यः कूलद्वयं यथा ।।१७।।

ततः कालवशादेव ह्यात्मज्ञानविवेकतः

उत्तराभिमुखो भूत्वा स्थानात्स्थानान्तरं क्रमात् ।।१८।।

ahaṃkārābhimānena jīvaḥ syāddhi sadāśivaḥ
sa cāvivekaprakṛtisaṅgatyā tatra muhyate (16)
nānāyoniśataṃ gatvā śete'sau vāsanāvasāt
vimokṣātsaṃcaratyeva matsyaḥ kūladvayaṃ yathā (17)
tataḥ kālavaśādeva hyātmajñānavivekataḥ
uttarābhimukho bhūtvā sthānātsthānāntaraṃ kramāt (18)

Vocabulary
dhi: indeed; *sadāśivaḥ*: Sadāśiva; *syāt jīvaḥ*: may become a jīva; *ahaṃkāra-abhimānena*: through the arrogance of ego; *ca*: and; *sa muhyate*: he can go astray; *saṅgatyā*: by mixing with; *prakṛti*: people; *aviveka*: lack discrimination; *gatvā*: having gone through; *nānā śatam*: many hundreds; *yoni*: wombs; *asau*: that; *śete*: remains; *avasāt*: helpless; *vāsana*: desire; *yathā*: just like; *matsyaḥ*: fish; *saṃcarati*: moving; *kūla-dvayam*: two banks of a river; *vimokṣāt*: away from liberation; *tataḥ*: then; *kāla-vaśāt*: through the rule of time; *vivekataḥ*: wise person; *uttara-abhimukhaḥ bhūtvā*: having faced north; *kramāt*: step by step; *sthānāt-sthāna-antaram*: from place to place; *ātma-jñāna*: knowledge of the ātman.

Translation
Indeed, [one who has reached] Sadāśiva may become a jīva through the arrogance of ego, and can go astray by mixing with people [who] lack discrimination.
Having gone through many hundreds [of] wombs, that [person] remains helpless with desires, just like a fish

moving [between] the two banks of a river away from liberation. Then, through the rule of time, the wise person, having faced north [and going] step by step from place to place, [gains] knowledge of the ātman.

Commentary

These verses emphasise the importance of *satsanga*, association with the wise and good. Even if the aspirant has reached sahasrāra cakra, the abode of the deity Sadāśiva, he can fall, becoming an ordinary person, if he takes pride in his status, and associates with people who are unable to discriminate between the *ahaṃkāra*, the small limited self, and the *paramātmā*, the Supreme Spirit. Because he has lived many lifetimes, there are many impressions on his mind, so he drifts from one transitory desire to another, unable to maintain the path to liberation. The verse uses the simile of the fish who is trapped between the two banks of the river instead of following it directly to the place where it merges with the ocean.

Eventually the person who is now wise turns and makes his way up the northern path, *uttarāyaṇa*, when the sun appears to move north. This is considered to be the path of illumination that leads towards liberation.

Verses 19 to 23: Yoga and Jñāna

मूर्धन्याधायात्मनः प्राणान्योगाभ्यासं स्थितश्चरन् ।
योगात्संजायते ज्ञानं ज्ञानाद्योगः प्रवर्तते ॥१९॥
योगज्ञानपरो नित्यं स योगी न प्रणश्यति ।
विकारस्थं शिवं पश्येद्विकारश्च शिवे न तु ॥२०॥
योगप्रकाशक्रं योगैर्ध्यायेच्चानन्यभावनः ।
योगज्ञाने न विद्येते तस्य भावो न सिध्यति ॥२१॥
तस्मादभ्यासयोगेन मनः प्राणान्निरोधयेत् ।
योगी निशितधारेण क्षुरेणैव निकृन्तयेत् ॥२२॥
शिखा ज्ञानमयी वृत्तिर्य माद्यष्टाङ्गसाधनैः ।
ज्ञानयोगः कर्मयोग इति योगो द्विधा मतः ॥२३॥

mūrdhanyādhāyātmanaḥ prāṇānyogābhyāsaṃ sthitaścaran yogātsaṃjāyate jñānaṃ jñānādyogaḥ pravartate (19)
yogajñānaparo nityaṃ sa yogī na praṇaśyati vikārasthaṃ śivaṃ paśyedvikāraśca śive na tu (20)
yogaprakāśakraṃ yogairdhyāyeccānanyabhāvanaḥ yogajñāne na vidyete tasya bhāvo na sidhyati (21)
tasmādabhyāsayogena manaḥ prāṇānnirodhayet yogī niśitadhāreṇa kṣureṇaiva nikṛntayet (22)
śikhā jñānamayī vṛttiryamādyaṣṭāṅgasādhanaiḥ jñānayogaḥ karmayoga iti yogo dvidhā mataḥ (23)

Vocabulary

ādhāya: having placed; *manaḥ*: mind; *sthitaḥ*: firmly; *mūrdhanya*: at the crown of the head; *prāṇān*: vital energies; *caran*: moved; *yoga-abhyāsam*: practice of yoga; *yogāt*: through yoga; *jñānam saṃjāyate*: wisdom arises; *jñānāt*: through wisdom; *yogaḥ pravartate*: yoga ensues; *yoga-jñāna-paraḥ*: both yoga and jñāna; *nityam*: constant; *sa yogī na praṇaśyati*: the yogin does not perish; *śivam paśyet*: he sees Śiva; *vikāra-stham*: where there are defects; *tu na vikāraḥ*:

but not defects; *śive*: in Śiva; *yogaiḥ*: through the practices of yoga; *dhyāyet*: he should meditate on; *yoga-prakāśakram*: light of yoga; *ca-ananya-bhāvanaḥ*: and with no other thought; *na vidyete yoga-jñāne*: if he does not have yoga and jñāna; *tasya bhāvaḥ*: his contemplation; *na sidhyati*: will not succeed; *tasmāt*: thus; *abhyāsa-yogena*: by the practice of yoga; *yogī nirodhayet*: yogin should control; *manaḥ*: mind; *prāṇāt*: with the force of vital nergy; *iva*: as if; *nikṛntayet*: he was cutting; *niśita-dhāreṇa kṣureṇa*: with the sharp blade of a knife; *sādhanaiḥ*: with the regular practice; *aṣṭāṅga*: eightfold path; *yama-ādi*: beginning with *yama*; *vṛttiḥ*: modifications of the mind; *mayī*: are transformed; *śikhā jñāna*: flame of jñāna; *iti yogaḥ mataḥ*: thus yoga is regarded as; *dvidhāḥ*: twofold; *jñāna-yogaḥ*: yoga of knowledge; *karma-yogaḥ*: yoga of action.

Translation

[When] the mind has been placed firmly at the crown of the head, [and] the vital energies moved [with] the practice of yoga, [then] through yoga, wisdom arises, and through wisdom yoga ensues. [When] both yoga and jñāna [are] constant, the yogin does not perish. He sees Śiva where there are defects, but not defects in Śiva. Through the practices of yoga, he should meditate on the light of yoga and with no other thought. If he does not have yoga and jñāna, his contemplation will not succeed. Thus, by the practice of yoga, the yogin should control the mind with the force of vital energy as if he was cutting with the sharp blade of a knife. With the regular practice [of] the eightfold path, beginning with yama, the modifications of the mind are transformed [into] the flame of jñāna. Thus yoga is regarded as twofold, the yoga of knowledge [and] the yoga of action.

Commentary

The regular and dedicated practice of yoga while the thoughts are fully absorbed in sahasrāra cakra gives rise to spiritual wisdom and union. The yogin dwells in the Supreme Light, seeing the perfection of Śiva who is pure consciousness, and seeing that pure consciousness within all imperfect beings. He should think of nothing else while meditating on the Supreme Light, and put all his energy into controlling the mind. Just as one false movement with a sharp knife can cause injury, so the diversion of thought can cause failure in meditation.

Jñāna Yoga, the path of intense self-enquiry, constantly asking 'who am I?' beyond the physical, mental, emotional and social self, is very difficult to follow by itself. The practices are *śravana*, hearing about the ātman or highest consciousness; *manana*, reflection, understanding; and *nididhyāsana*, deep meditation. Ramana Mahārṣi, the well-known *jñāna yogi*, was already established in dhyāna, and so was able to follow that path alone. Therefore, the verse says, it is to be combined with the paths of Kriyā Yoga or Karma Yoga.

Through the eightfold path of yoga one can purify the mind and attain jñāna. The eight limbs of the eightfold path are *yama*, external observances, moral interaction with others, *niyama*, internal disciplines, *āsana*, steady postures, *prāṇāyāma*, breath control and expansion of energy, *pratyāhāra*, disassociation from the senses, *dhāraṇā*, concentration, *dhyāna*, meditation, and *samādhi*, transcendental consciousness.

'In dhyāna there is total identification and merger of the mind into samādhi. In jñāna there is full experiential knowledge of the merger. So jñāna and dhyāna combined give the experience of samādhi.'[13]

Verses 24 to 28a: Twofold Yoga

क्रियायोगमथेदानीं शृणु ब्राह्मणसत्तम् ।

अव्याकुलस्य चित्तस्य बन्धनं विषये क्वचित् ।।२४।।

यत्संयोगो द्विजश्रेष्ठ स च द्वैविध्यमश्नुते ।

कर्म कर्तव्यमित्येव विहितेष्वेव कर्मसु ।।२५।।

बन्धनं मनसा नित्यं कर्मयोगः स उच्यते ।

यत्तु चित्तस्य सततमर्थे श्रेयसि बन्धनम् ।।२६।।

ज्ञानयोगः स विज्ञेयः सर्वसिद्धिकरः शिवः ।

यस्योक्तलक्षणे योगे द्विविधेऽप्यव्ययं मनः ।।२७।।

स याति परमं श्रेयो मोक्षलक्षणमञ्जसा ।२८।

kriyāyogamathedānīṃ śṛṇu brāhmaṇasattam avyākulasya cittasya bandhanaṃ viṣaye kvacit (24)
yatsaṃyogo dvijaśreṣtha sa ca dvaividhyamaśnute karma kartavyamityeva vihiteṣveva karmasu (25)
bandhanaṃ manasā nityaṃ karmayogaḥ sa ucyate yattu cittasya satatamarthe śreyasi bandhanam (26)
jñānayogaḥ sa vijñeyaḥ sarvasiddhikaraḥ śivaḥ yasyoktalakṣaṇe yoge dvividhe'pyavyayaṃ manaḥ (27)
sa yāti paramaṃ śreyo mokṣalakṣaṇamañjasā (28a)

Vocabulary

brāhmaṇa-sattam: o most venerable Brāhmaṇa; *śṛṇu*: listen to; *atha idānīm*: now; *kriya-yogam*: kriyā yoga; *kvacit*: now; *viṣaye*: in its subject matter; *bandhanam*: restraint; *avyākulasya cittasya*: of the confused mind; *dvija-śreṣtha*: o excellent Twice-born; *yat-saṃyogaḥ*: whatever combination; *sa aśnute*: one can reach; *dvaividhyam*: twofold state; *karma kartavyam*: duty [and] action; *karmasu*: when . . . are done; *vihiteṣu*: as prescribed; *karmayogaḥ*: karma yoga; *sa ucyate*: it is said; *nityam*: always; *bandhanam*: control; *manasā*: of the mind; *arthe*: by means of; *yat satatam- bandhanam*: this continuous control; *śreyasi*: benefit; *cittasya*: for the mind; *sa vijñeyaḥ*: whoever knows; *jñāna-yogaḥ*: jñāna yoga; *sarva-*

siddhi-karaḥ śivaḥ: has all the powers of Śiva; *yasya ukta*: thus it is said; *lakṣaṇe*: if the aim; *dvividhe yoge*: twofold yoga; *api*: then; *manaḥ*: mind; *avyayam*: imperishable; *śreyaḥ*: accomplished one; *mokṣa-lakṣaṇam*: aim [of] liberation; *añjasā*: instantly; *yāti*: goes to; *paramam*: Absolute.

Translation
O most venerable Brāhmaṇa, listen now to [the meaning of] kriyā yoga. Now in its subject matter [there is] restraint of the confused mind. O excellent Twice-born, whatever combination [one uses], one can reach the twofold state, when duty [and] action are done as prescribed [in the scriptures]. Karma yoga, it is said, always [has] control of the mind. By means of this continuous control, [there is] benefit for the mind. Whoever knows jñāna yoga, has all the powers of Śiva. Thus it is said if the aim [is] the twofold yoga, then the mind [is] imperishable. The accomplished one, [whose] aim is liberation, instantly goes to the Absolute.

Commentary
Kriyā Yoga, the yoga of spiritual action, has practices which gradually raise the *kuṇḍalinī* energy from mūlādhāra to sahasrāra cakra. *Bandhas*, *kumbhaka* and *khecarī mudrā* are some of the practices. Through these practices the mind is transformed from a state of confusion to clarity.

Karma Yoga, yoga of action, is the yoga of dynamic meditation, where the normal everyday activites of body and mind are combined with meditative awareness. 'Do your duty without any attachment to the fruits of your work, for only by acting without attachment can you reach the Divine.' [14]

Swami Niranjan defines *Jñānakarma Yoga*, which is the theme of Chapter 4 of *Bhagavad Gīta*, as 'recognition and acceptance of the situation combined with the necessary effort to go beyond that'.[15]

Both combinations, Kriyā Yoga with Jñāna Yoga, or Karma Yoga with Jñāna Yoga, lead to liberation. A *jñāna yogi*, having 'all the powers of Śiva', has reached *kaivalya*, final emancipation, the state of consciousness beyond duality.

Verses 28b to 32a: Eightfold Path

देहेन्द्रियेषु वैराग्यं यम इत्युच्यते बुधैः ॥२८॥
अनुरक्तिः परे तत्त्वे सततं नियमः स्मृतः ।
सर्ववस्तून्युदासीनभावमासनमुत्तमम् ॥२९॥
जगत्सर्वमिदं मिथ्याप्रतीतिः प्राणसंयमः ।
चित्तस्यान्तर्मुखभावः प्रत्याहारस्तु सत्तम ॥३०॥
चित्तस्य निश्चलीभावो धारणा धारणां विदुः ।
सोऽहं चिन्मात्रमेवेति चिन्तनं ध्यानमुच्यते ॥३१॥
ध्यानस्य विस्मृतिः सम्यक्समाधिरभिधीयते ।३२।

dehendriyeṣu vairāgyaṃ yama ityucyate budhaiḥ (28b)
anuraktiḥ pare tattve satataṃ niyamaḥ smṛtaḥ
sarvavastūnyudāsīnabhāvamāsanamuttamaṃ (29)
jagatsarvamidaṃ mithyāpratītiḥ prāṇasaṃyamaḥ
cittasyāntarmukhabhāvaḥ pratyāhārastu sattama (30)
cittasya niścalībhāvo dhāraṇā dhāraṇāṃ viduḥ
so'haṃ cinmātrameveti cintanaṃ dhyānamucyate (31)
dhyānasya vismṛtiḥ samyaksamādhirabhidhīyate (32a)

Vocabulary

iti-ucyate: thus it is said; *budhaiḥ*: by the wise; *yamaḥ*: self-restraint; *vairāgyam*: detachment; *deha-indriyeṣu*: from the sense organs of the body; *niyamaḥ*: *niyama*, personal disciplines; *smṛtaḥ*: is described as; *satatam*: continuous; *anuraktiḥ*: devotion; *pare tattve*: to the transcendental essence; *bhāvam*: attitude; *udāsīna*: non-attachment; *sarva-vastūni*: all things; *uttamam āsanam*: supreme *āsana*; *prāṇa-saṃyamaḥ*: control of vital airs; *mithyā-pratītiḥ*: false belief; *idam sarvam jagat*: this whole world; *tu pratyāhāraḥ*: now *pratyahara*, withdrawal of the senses; *sattama*: first; *antarmukhabhāvaḥ*: introversion; *cittasya*: of the mind; *niścalībhāvaḥ dhāraṇā*: fixed concentration; *cittasya*: on the mind; *viduḥ dhāraṇām*: is known as *dhāraṇā*; *cinmātram*: pure intelligence; *iti eva*: is really; *cintanam*: thought; *so'ham*: I am this; *ucyate dhyāna*: this is called *dhyana*, meditation; *vismṛtiḥ*: loss of memory;

dhyānasya: in dhyana; *samyak*: duly; *abhidhīyate*: is expressed as; *samādhiḥ*: *samādhi*, self-realisation.

Translation

Thus it is said by the wise that *yama* [is] detachment from the sense organs of the body. *Niyama* is described as continuous devotion to the transcendental essence. The attitude [of] non-attachment [to] all things [is] the supreme *āsana*. [In] the control of vital airs [one understands] the false belief [in] this whole world. Now *pratyāhāra* is first introversion of the mind. Fixed concentration on the mind is known as *dhāraṇā*. Pure intelligence is really the thought 'That I am'. This is called *dhyāna*. Loss of memory [of the previous states] in dhyāna is duly expressed as *samādhi*.

Commentary

The foundation and first stage of the eightfold path is *yama*, moral and ethical interaction with others, which surpasses sensory pleasures and gratification. *Niyama* are the inner disciplines necessary for spiritual development. The *Yoga Sūtras* define *āsana* as a steady comfortable sitting position.[16] In this verse *āsana*, posture, means how one carries oneself in the world with discrimination and detachment. Once one has control of all the vital energies through *prāṇāyāma*, one understands that everything comes from *mahāprāṇa*, the cosmic unmanifest *prāṇa*. When the mind is first introverted, it withdraws and disassociates from the five senses of sound, touch, sight, taste and smell. This process is called *pratyāhāra*. Having withdrawn the senses, one is able to concentrate on a symbol of higher consciousness, given by the guru or of one's own choice. This is called *dhāraṇā*. Then keeping the mind on the thought '*so'ham*', 'so' representing cosmic consciousness, and 'ham' individual consciousness, leads spontaneously to deep meditation, *dhyāna*.

When there is no thought in the mind, only pure awareness, this is the state of samādhi.

Verses 32b to 34a: Yama and Niyama

अहिंसा सत्यमस्तेयं ब्रह्मचर्यं दयार्ज्वम् ।।३२।।
क्षमा धृतिर्मिताहारः शौचं चेति यमा दश ।
तपः सन्तुष्टिरास्तिक्यं दानमाराधनं हरेः ।।३३।।
वेदान्तश्रवणं चैव ह्रीर्मतिश्च जपो व्रतम् । इति ।३४।

ahiṃsā satyamasteyaṃ brahmacaryaṃ dayārjvam (32b)
kṣamā dhṛtirmitāhāraḥ śaucaṃ ceti yamā daśa
tapaḥ santuṣṭirāstikyaṃ dānamārādhanaṃ hareḥ (33)
vedāntaśravaṇaṃ caiva hrīrmatiśca japo vratam iti (34a)

Vocabulary

daśa yamāḥ iti: ten yamas are; *ahiṃsā*: non-violence; *satyam*: truth; *asteyam*: honesty; *brahmacaryam*: celibacy; *dayā*: kindness; *ārjavam*: straightforwardness; *kṣamā*: patience; *dhṛtiḥ*: steadiness; *mitāhāraḥ*: diet; *ca śaucam*: and cleanliness; *tapaḥ*: self-discipline; *santuṣṭiḥ*: complete contentment; *āstikyam*: theism; *dānam*: generosity; *ārādhanaṃ hareḥ*: worship of the Divine; *vedānta-śravaṇam*: listening to the Vedas; *hṛīḥ*: remorse; *matiḥ*: faith; *japaḥ*: mantra repetition; *ca vratam*: and resolution.

Translation

The ten yamas are non-violence, truth, honesty, celibacy, kindness, straightforwardness, patience, steadiness, diet and cleanliness. [The niyamas] are self-discipline, complete contentment, theism, generosity, worship of the Divine, listening to the Vedas, remorse, faith, mantra repetition and resolution.

Commentary

The ten yamas are external observances, that is, moral interactions with others. *Ahiṃsā* means non-harming in action, speech and thought. It is an absence of violence from within. Satyam, truth, means truthfulness in speech,

with the awareness of that which is correct and true, without distortion by *saṃskaras* and *vrittis*.
Its deeper meaning is awareness of that which is unchanging and permanent, the True Reality, Brahman. The literal meaning of asteya is not cheating or stealing. It also means honesty with ourselves about our motives, opinions and actions in our life, and in our dealings with others. *Brahmacarya* is absolute control of sensual impulses. It literally means one who moves in the highest consciousness. *Dayā* is kindness, an inner quality which expresses itself in everyday life. *Ārjavam* means to be straightforward with oneself, and with all of one's associations and dealings in life in thought, speech and behaviour. Such a person has integrity, is honest, not devious and is free from crookedness or deceit. *Kṣamā* is patience and endurance. Whoever can remain calm, accepting how things unfold, without losing patience, is in control of the mind and senses. *Dhṛti*, equanimity, is the ability to maintain a firm, calm and balanced state of mind and to remain true to one's principles, even in the midst of turbulence all around. *Mitāhāra* is moderation in food. The food of a yogin should be easily and quickly digested, so that the body remains light and fit for yoga practices. *Śauca*
is cleanliness in body and mind.

The ten niyamas are internal disciplines, which allow the practitioner to gain control over the senses and manage the mind at a deeper level.

Tapas is the practice of self-discipline and austerity (not self-abuse), so that one can bear all difficulties on the spiritual path. *Santoṣa* means that inner contentment where one is satisfied with one's situation, living in the present, thus reducing desires and the craving aspect of the mind. *Āstikya* is deep faith in the higher reality, by listening to and studying the vedic texts. *Dāna* means donation, gift, unconditional giving. *Īśvara puja*, worship of the highest consciousness, which is unmanifest and indestructible.

Siddhānta śravaṇa, listening to and reflecting on the meaning and teachings of Vedānta. *Hrī* means shame in the sense of remorse. *Mati* is understanding and faith in the paths of action prescribed by the Vedas.

Mantra repetition (called *japa*) [is] constant practice of the sacred mantra given by the guru or not contrary to the Vedas. *Vrata*, a vow, is a sincere commitment to adhere to the yamas and niyamas.[17]

Verses 34b & 40: Āsana: Svastika Gomukha Vīra Padma

आसानानि तदङ्गानि स्वस्तिकादीनि वै द्विज ॥३४॥
वर्ण्यन्ते स्वस्तिकं पादतलयोरुभयोरपि ।
पूर्वोत्तरे जानुनी द्वे कृत्वासनमुदीरितम् ॥३५॥
सव्ये दक्षिणगुल्फं तु पृष्ठपार्श्वे नियोजयेत् ।
दक्षिणेऽपि तथा सव्यं गोमुखं गोमुखं यथा ॥३६॥
एकं चरणमन्यस्मिन्नूरावारोपि निश्चलः ।
आस्ते यदिदमेनोघ्नं वीरासनमुदीरितम् ॥३७॥
गुदं नियम्य गुल्फाभ्यां व्युत्क्रमेण समाहितः ।
योगासनं भवेदेतदिति योगविदो विदुः ॥३८॥
ऊर्ध्वोरुपरि वै धत्ते यदा पादतले उभे ।
पद्मासनं भवेदेतत्सर्वव्याधिविषापहम् ॥३९॥
पद्मासनं सुसंस्थाप्य तदङ्गुष्ठद्वयं पुनः ।
व्युत्क्रमेणैव हस्ताभ्यां बद्धपद्मासनं भवेत् ॥४०॥

āsanāni tadaṅgāni svastikādīni vai dvija (34b)
varṇyante svastikaṃ pādatalayorubhayorapi
pūrvottare jānunī dve kṛtvāsanamudīritam (35)
savye dakṣiṇagulphaṃ tu pṛṣṭhapārśve niyojayet
dakṣiṇe'pi tathā savyaṃ gomukhaṃ gomukhaṃ yathā (36)
ekaṃ caraṇamanyasminnūrāvāropi niścalaḥ
āste yadidamenoghraṃ vīrāsanamudīritam (37)
gudaṃ niyamya gulphābhyāṃ vyutkrameṇa samāhitaḥ
yogāsanaṃ bhavedetaditi yogavido viduḥ (38)
ūrdhvorupari vai dhatte yadā pādatale ubhe
padmāsanaṃ bhavedetatsarvavyādhiviṣāpaham (39)
padmāsanaṃ susaṃsthāpya tadaṅguṣṭhadvayaṃ punaḥ
vyutkrameṇaiva hastābhyāṃ baddhapadmāsanaṃ bhavet (40)

Vocabulary

dvija: O Brāhmaṇa (*lit.* twice-born); *tad*: then; *aṅgāni āsana*: branches of *āsana*; *svastika-ādīni*: *svastika* and others;

varṇyante: are described; *kṛtvā*: placing; *ubhayoḥ pāda-talayoḥ*: both soles of the feet; *pūrvottare*: in front of and above; *dve jānunī*: two knees; *udīritam*: is called; *svastikam āsanam*: *svastikāsana*, auspicious pose; *tu*: now; *niyojayet*: placing; *dakṣiṇa-gulpham*: right ankle; *savye*: on the left; *pṛṣṭha-pārśve*: beside the back; *api tathā*: and similarly; *savyam*: left; *dakṣiṇe*: on the right; *gomukham*: cow-face; *āste*: if one is seated; *niścalaḥ*: firmly; *ekam caraṇam*: each foot; *anyasmin-ūrāvāḥ*: on opposite thighs; *idam udīritam vīrāsanam*: this is called *vīrāsana*, hero pose; *niyamya*: contracted; *gudam*: contracted; *samāhitaḥ*: has been pressed; *gulphābhyām*: by both ankles; *vyutkrameṇa*: by turning up; *etat bhavet yogāsanam*: this is *yogāsana*; *iti viduḥ*: so say the wise; *yoga-vidaḥ*: who know yoga; *yadā*: when; *ubhe pāda-tale*: both soles of the feet; *dhatte*: are placed; *-upari*: upwards; *ūrdhvoḥ*: on the thighs; *bhavet padmāsanam*: this is *padmāsana*, lotus pose; *etat*: this; *viṣāpaham*: antidote; *sarva-vyādhi*: all disease; *susaṃsthāpya punaḥ padmāsanam*: positioned again in padmāsana; *aṅguṣṭha-dvayam*: two big toes; *vyutkrameṇa*: turned up; *hastābhyām*: by the hands; *bhavet baddhapadmāsanam*: this is *baddha-padmāsana*, bound lotus pose.

Translation

O Brāhmaṇa, then the branches of *āsana*, *svastika* and others, are described. Placing both soles of the feet in front of and above the two knees is called *svastikāsana*. Now placing the right ankle on the left beside the back, and similarly the left on the right [is] *gomukha*, the cow-face [pose]. If one is firmly seated, each foot on the opposite thigh, this is called *vīrāsana*. [When] the contracted anus has been pressed by both ankles, by turning [them] up, this is *yogāsana*. So say the wise who know yoga. When both soles of the feet are placed upwards on the thighs, this is *padmāsana*. This [is] an antidote to all disease.

Positioned again in padmāsana, the two big toes turned up by the hands, this is *baddha-padmāsana*.

Commentary
The postures described in Verses 34b to 52 have physical, mental and energic benefits, and many people perform them just for these benefits. However the main purpose of these postures is to enable us to sit longer in meditation without discomfort or having to move. For this reason, the whole progression of yoga āsana developed, including āsanas, for every possible type of bodily movement: forward, backward, sideways, upward, inverted, and balancing. When the progression of āsana is properly mastered, the aspirant should be able to remove the toxins, tensions and stiffness from the body, so that sitting in one posture for a long period of time becomes possible for the purpose of meditation.

Svastikāsana
'*Svasti*' means 'auspicious'; the suffix '*ka*' means 'belonging to'. So *svastika* literally means an 'auspicious object'. The *svastika*, auspicious object, has been portrayed as a cross with arms of equal length bent at right angles, usually in the clockwise direction, imitating the daily course of the Sun (in the Northern Hemisphere). It has been a symbol of prosperity and good fortune for thousands of years in the ancient and modern world. In India it is still widely used by Hindus, Jains and Buddhists. A common analogy of the swastika is that its four limbs represent the four directions of the world, which have one common centre, consciousness. Therefore, this pose can be considered as the one most auspicious for realising the unity of all existence. In Nazi Germany this symbol was distorted both in appearance, the arms of the cross being oblique, and in meaning, a symbol of violence and racism.

Svastikāsana helps relieve varicose veins and sore muscles, and diminish fluid retention in the legs. Suṣumnā nāḍī, the central energy flow in the spine, is stimulated to move from mūlādhāra cakra at the base of the spine towards sahasrāra cakra at the crown of the head. This is an easier version of *siddhāsana*.

Do not sit in this position if you have sciatica or sacral injury.

Gomukhāsana

'*Go*' means 'cow' and '*mukha*' means 'face'. This posture bears similarity to the face of a cow. The cow is considered sacred for several reasons. Sri Krishna, the avatar, was a cow herder. The cow gives many benefits without asking for anything in return. She provides nutrition and energy in the form of milk. Her dung is used as a fertiliser, as it is rich in minerals. Cow dung is saved and used for fuel, as it is high in methane, and can generate heat and electricity. Many villagers use a mixture made of mud and cow dung either to make bricks for their homes or as an insulation from extreme hot and cold temperatures by plastering the walls with it. Vedic sacred fire ceremonies, called *yajña* or *agnihotra*, use cow dung and ghee as fuel, which has been found to purify the air, having anti-pollutant and anti-radiation effects on the environment.

If you can hold gomukhāsana for at least ten minutes, you will notice all fatigue, tension and anxiety decreasing. This posture also stimulates the kidneys, relieves back pain, and relaxes the shoulders, neck. It removes cramps in the legs, making the muscles malleable. The position of the arms straightens the back and opens up the chest, improving posture. Keep your attention on the natural breath and on *ājñā cakra* at the eyebrow centre or *anāhata cakra* at the heart centre.

Be careful of the knees when bending and straightening the legs. Legs can be stretched out in front if the knees are weak, injured or stiff.

Vīrāsana

In this pose the left upper arm rests on the knee of the left leg, so that the chin can rest in the palm of the left hand. The eyes are lightly closed. The meditator in this posture seems to be contemplating on some worldly or spiritual matter. That is why the posture is also known as the thinker's or philosopher's pose. It is said to be named after *Mahāvīra* (Great Hero) which is another name for *Hanumān*, the monkey god in the *Ramāyana*, who embodied the heroic qualities of courage, strong character and selflessness.

Vīrāsana is beneficial for the kidneys, liver, reproductive and abdominal organs. It helps mind and body to relax. Fix your attention on ājñā cakra at the eyebrow centre, developing the power of concentration and clarity of mind.

Yogāsana

Yogāsana is a general word for a seated posture typically used for meditation, such as a basic cross-legged position.

Padmāsana

Padmāsana is named after the lotus flower, because the lotus has its roots in the mud, and submerges every night into the muddy water, then rises and blooms again the next morning, its petals pristine and unsullied. Like the lotus, we can remain unsullied by obstacles and painful experiences, using them to advance spiritually.

If not forced into this posture, the body can be held steady for quite some time, calming the mind, and entering deep states of meditation. The lotus posture directs the flow of prāṇa from mūlādhāra towards sahasrāra cakra. The pressure on the lower spine relaxes the nervous spine, and increases the blood flow to the abdominal area, stimulating the digestive process.

Do not sit in this position if you have sciatica, sacral injury, weak, injured or stiff knees as kneecaps and ligaments can be damaged.

One should not force the body into *padmāsana.* Often children under the age of seven sit naturally and easily in this lotus pose, as they sit mainly on the floor at school. From the age of seven, they spend more time sitting in chairs, thereby losing some flexibility.

Baddha Padmāsana

Baddha Padmāsana, *baddha* meaning 'bound', is a variation of padmāsana, where the arms are placed behind the back and crossed. The body leans forward slightly and the shoulders stretched back, so that the right hand can clasp the right big toe, and the left hand the left big toe. Then the body leans forward with the aim of bringing the forehead to the floor.

This pose alleviates pain in the shoulders, arms and back, and massages the internal organs. It is a practice used to awaken kuṇḍalinī. Again, one should not force the body into this posture.

Verses 41 and 46: Āsana: Kukkuṭa Kūrma Dhanur Bhadra Mukta

पद्मासनं सुसंस्थाप्य जानूर्वोरन्तरे करौ ।
निवेश्य भूमावातिष्ठेद्व्योमस्थः कुक्कुटासनः ।।४१।।
कुक्कुटासनबन्धस्थो दोर्भ्यां संबध्य कन्धरम् ।
शेते कूर्मवदुत्तान एतदुत्तानकूर्मकम् ।।४२।।
पादाङ्गुष्ठौ तु पाणिभ्यां गृहीत्वा श्रवणावधि ।
धनुराकर्णकाकृष्टं धनुरासनमीरितम् ।।४३।।
सीवनीं गुल्फदेशाभ्यां निपीड्य व्युत्क्रमेण तु ।
प्रसार्य जानुनोर्हस्तावासनं सिंहरूपकम् ।।४४।।
गुल्फौ च वृषणस्याधाः सीविन्युभयपार्श्वयोः ।
निवेश्य पादौ हस्ताभ्यां बध्वा भद्रासनं भवेत् ।।४५।।
सीवनीपार्श्वमुभयं गुल्फाभ्यां व्युत्क्रमेण तु ।
निपीड्यासनमेतच्च मुक्तासनमुदीरितम् ।।४६।।

padmāsanaṃ susaṃsthāpya jānūrvorantare karau niveśya bhūmāvātiṣṭhedvyomasthaḥ kukkuṭāsanaḥ (41)
kukkuṭāsanabandhastho dorbhyāṃ saṃbadhya kandharam śete kūrmavaduttāna etaduttānakūrmakam (42)
pādāṅguṣṭhau tu pāṇibhyāṃ gṛhītvā śravaṇāvadhi dhanurākarṇakākṛṣṭaṃ dhanurāsanamīritam (43)
sīvanīṃ gulphadeśābhyāṃ nipīḍya vyutkrameṇa prasārya jānunorhastāvāsanaṃ siṃharūpakam (44)
gulphau ca vṛṣaṇasyādhāḥ sīvinyubhayapārśvayoḥ niveśya pādau hastābhyāṃ badhvā bhadrāsanaṃ bhavet (45)
sīvanīpārśvamubhayaṃ gulphābhyāṃ vyutkrameṇa tu nipīḍyāsanametacca muktāsanamudīritam (46)

Vocabulary

susaṃsthāpya: positioned in; *padmāsanam*: padmāsana, lotus pose; *karau*: putting; *jānūrvoḥ-antare*: inside the knees; *niveśya*: placing; *bhūmāva*: on the ground; *ātiṣṭhet*: one should hold; *kukkuṭāsanaḥ*: *kukkuṭāsana*, rooster pose; *bandhasthaḥ kukkuṭāsana*: locked in kukkuṭāsana; *saṃbadhya*: having bound; *kandharam*: neck; *dorbhyām*: with the shoulders; *śete*: resting; *uttāna*: spread out; *kūrmavat*: like a tortoise; *etat*: this; *uttāna-kūrmakam*: stretched out tortoise; *gṛhītvā*: pulling; *pādāṅguṣṭhau*: feet; *śravaṇāvadhi*: up to the ears; *pāṇibhyām*: with the hands; *karṇakā*: legs spread out; *kṛṣṭam*: drawn up; *dhanurā*: like a bow; *īrita*: is called; *dhanurāsanam*: *dhanurāsana*, bow pose; *nipīḍya*: pressing; *sīvanīm*: genitals; *gulpha-deśābhyām*: parts of the ankles; *vyutkrameṇa*: upturned; *prasārya*: extending; *āsanam*: posture; *hastau*: hands; *jānunoḥ*: on the knees; *siṃha-rūpakam*: form of the lion; *niveśya*: placing; *gulphau*: ankles; *vṛṣaṇasya-adhāḥ*: below the testicles; *sīvini-ubhaya-pārśvayoḥ*: on both sides of the buttocks; *badhvā*: holding; *pādau*: feet; *hastābhyām*: with the hands; *bhavet bhadrāsanam*: is *bhadrāsana*, gracious pose; *nipīḍya*: pressing; *sīvanī-pārśvam-ubhayam*: both sides of the genitals; *gulphābhyāṃ vyutkrameṇa*: with the ankles turned up; *ca etat āsanam*: and this āsana; *udīritam*: is called; *muktāsanam*: *muktāsana*, liberated pose.

Translation

Positioned in padmāsana, putting [the hands] inside the knees, placing [them] on the ground [and] locked in *kukkuṭāsana*, one should hold kukkuṭāsana in the air. Having bound the neck with the shoulders, resting spread out like a tortoise, this [is] the stretched-out tortoise [pose], *kūrmāsana*. Pulling the feet up to the ears with the hands, the legs spread out [and] drawn up like a bow, is called *dhanurāsana*. Pressing the genitals with parts of the upturned ankles, extending the posture with hands on the knees, [is] the form of the lion, *siṃhāsana*. Placing the ankles below the testicles on both sides of the buttocks [and] holding the feet with the hands, is *bhadrāsana*.

Pressing both sides of the genitals with the ankles turned up, this āsana is called **muktāsana**.

Commentary

Kukkuṭāsana

Kukkuṭa means 'rooster'. The upper body needs to be strong to perform this posture. Once in the posture it is further strengthened. It also loosens the leg muscles. It stimulates mūlādhāra cakra, preparing for the awakening of the kuṇḍalinī.

Kūrmāsana

Kūrma means 'tortoise'. This posture tones all the abdominal organs, and improves circulation in the spine, relaxing head and neck and instilling a feeling of inner calm. The Bhagavad Gītā compares sense withdrawal (*pratyāhāra*) to the wise tortoise who withdraws its limbs from external danger. [18]

Dhanurāsana

Dhanu means 'bow'. This posture improves the functioning of the digestive, eliminative and reproductive organs. It improves blood circulation and respiration, and removes stiffness from ligaments and muscles. It is not for people who have high blood pressure, a weak heart, hernia or ulcers.

Bhadrāsana

The word *bhadra* means 'gentle', 'gracious' or 'blessed'. This āsana automatically induces mūla bandha, the perineal lock, and is used for the awakening of mūlādhāra cakra, the root psychic centre. The practitioner should keep the awareness on mūlādhāra cakra and the natural breath or the nose tip. For this reason, it is also called *mūlabandhāsana* in some of the classical texts. It is an important posture for the conservation of sexual energy, and helps to tone the reproductive and eliminatory organs. Therefore, it keeps the body free from toxic buildup in the lower regions and helps to avert disease. Bhadrāsana is an excellent meditation pose for the advanced practitioner, whose knees, ankles and feet are very flexible.

Muktāsana

Muktāsana, the liberated pose, is another name for *siddhāsana*. The left heel is under the anus, the right heel above it. It can be practised by both sexes.

Verses 47 to 52: Āsana: Māyūra Matsya Siddha Paścimottāna Sukha

अवष्टब्य धरां सम्यक्तलाभ्यां हस्तयोर्द्वयोः ।
कूर्परौ नाभिपार्श्वे तु स्थापयित्वा मयूरवत् ।।४७।।
समुन्नतशिरः पादं मयूरासनमिष्यते ।
वामोरुमूले दक्षाङ्घ्रिं जान्वोर्वेष्टिपाणिना ।।४८।।
वामेन वामाङ्गुष्ठं तु गृहीतं मत्स्यपीठकम् ।
योनिं वामेन संपीड्य मेढ्रादुपरि दक्षिनम् ।।४९।।
ऋजुकायः समासीनः सिद्धासनमुदीरितम् ।
प्रसार्य भुवि पादौ तु दोर्भ्यामङ्गुष्ठमादरात् ।।५०।।
जानूपरि ललाटं तु पश्चिमोत्तानमुच्यते ।
येन प्रकारेण सुखं धार्यं च जायते ।।५१।।
तत्सुखासनमित्युक्तमशक्रस्तत्समाचरेत् ।
आसनं विजितं येन जितं तेन जगत्त्रयम् ।।५२।।

avaṣṭabya dharāṃ samyaktalābhyāṃ hastayordvahoḥ
kūrparau nābhipārśve tu sthāpayitvā mayūravat (47)
samunnataśiraḥ pādaṃ mayūrāsanamiṣyate
vāmorumūle dakṣāṅghriṃ jānvorveṣṭipāṇinā (48)
vāmena vāmāṅguṣṭhaṃ tu gṛhītaṃ matsyapīṭhakam
yoniṃ vāmena saṃpīḍya meḍhrādupari dakṣinam (49)
ṛjukāyaḥ samāsīnaḥ siddhāsanamudīritam
prasārya bhuvi pādau tu dorbhyāmaṅguṣṭhamādarāt (50)
jānūpari lalāṭaṃ tu paścimottānamucyate
yena prakāreṇa sukhaṃ dhāryaṃ ca jāyate (51)
tatsukhāsanamityuktamaśakrastatsamācaret
āsanaṃ vijitaṃ yena jitaṃ tena jagattrayam (52)

Vocabulary

avaṣṭabya: grasping; *dharām*: holding; *talābhyām*: soles of the *feet; samyak*: together; *hastayoḥ-dvahoḥ*: with two hands; *tu sthāpayitvā*: now placing; *kūrparau*: elbows; *nābhi-pārśve*: near the navel; *mayūra-vat*: like a peacock; *śiraḥ*:

head; *pādam*: feet; *samunnata*: raised; *iṣyate*: one moves into; *mayūrāsanam*: *mayūrāsana*, peacock pose; *jānvoḥ-veṣṭi*: knees bent; *dakṣa-aṅghrim*: right foot; *vāmena pāṇinā*: with the left hand; *mule*: on top; *vāma-uru*: left thigh; *tu gṛhītam*: now grasping; *vāma-aṅguṣṭham*: left big toe; *matsya-pīṭhakam*: *matsyāsana*, fish pose; *saṃpīḍya*: pressing; *yonim*: vulva; *vāmena*: with the left; *dakṣinam*: right; *upari*: above; *meḍhrāt*: genitals; *samāsīnaḥ*: seated; *ṛju-kāyaḥ*: straight body; *siddhāsanam-udīritam*: is called *siddhāsana*, accomplished pose; *pādau*: legs; *prasārya*: stretched out; *bhuvi*: on the floor; *ādarāt*: carefully; *aṅguṣṭham*: big toes; *dorbhyām*: by the forearms; *tu lalātam*: then the forehead; *jānu-upari*: above the knees; *paścimottānam-ucyate*: [this] is called *paścimottānasana*; *sukham*: comfortable; *dhāryam*: stable; *uktam*: is called; *sukhāsanam*: *sukhāsana*, easy pose; *aśakraḥ*: unable; *samācaret*: practise; *yena prakāreṇa*: in whichever way; *yena vijitam āsanam*: whoever has conquered āsana; *tena*: therefore; *jitam*: has conquered; *jagat-trayam*: three worlds.

Translation

Grasping [and] holding the soles of the feet together with two hands, [and] now placing the elbows near the navel like a peacock, head [and] feet raised, one moves into *mayūrāsana*. Knees bent, [place] the right foot with the left hand on top [of] the left thigh, now grasping the left big toe, [this is] *matsyāsana*. Pressing the vulva with the left [foot], the right [foot] above the genitals, seated [with] a straight body, is called *siddhāsana*. Legs stretched out on the floor, carefully [hold] the big toes by the forearms, then the forehead above the knees. [This] is called *paścimottānāsana*. A comfortable and stable [posture] is called *sukhāsana*. [It is for those who are] unable [to] practise [an āsana] in whichever way. Whoever has conquered āsana, has therefore conquered the three worlds.

Commentary

Māyūrāsana

Mayurāsana, the peacock pose, is mentioned in this upaniṣad and in many classical texts on yoga, due to its powerful influence on the *maṇipura cakra* and the digestive system. The other postures mentioned in this section are all sitting postures. The purpose of including this major āsana here may have been for health reasons. The Indian subcontinent is hot and humid for many months of the year. Continuous heat and humidity affect the metabolism, causing toxins and bacteria to proliferate.

Mayurāsana massages the abdominal organs and stimulates the intestinal peristalsis. It removes toxins and develops mental and physical balance. Therefore the practitioner should keep the awareness on both maintaining balance and maṇipura cakra.

'Just as a peacock can kill and digest snakes without being affected by the poison, this āsana enables the practitioner to digest and metabolise the residual toxins and poisons in the body.'[19]

Do not attempt this posture if you have any heart ailment, hernia, peptic ulcers, back problems or if you have any sign of illness or physical weakness, or if you are pregnant.

Matsyāsana

Matsya means 'fish'. This posture stretches the intestines and abdominal organs. It encourages deep breathing, so it is good for relieving asthama and bronchitis. It regulates the thyroid gland and stimulates the thymus gland, boosting the immune system. It increases the blood circulation in the pelvic organs, benefiting the reproductive system. **Do not** attempt this posture if you have high blood pressure, any heart ailment, hernia, peptic or duodenal ulcer, if you have any sign of illness or physical weakness, or if you are pregnant.

Siddhāsana

The word *siddha* means 'accomplished' or 'perfected'. It refers to one, who is accomplished in yoga through the mastery of this pose. *Siddhāsana* and *padmāsana* are the two most important meditative poses. The other meditation poses are modifications, some of which may be practised more easily and others that are even more difficult. The body is firmly locked in siddhāsana and the feet are less likely to become numb. While padmāsana aims at achieving total balance of the prāṇas for the awakening of suṣumnā, siddhāsana activates the lower centres and redirects the reproductive energy upward to the brain to be used for higher meditation.

Siddhāsana stops the blood pressure from falling too low, and awakens ājña cakra, the psychic centre at the mid-brain, due to the connection between mūlādhāra and ājñā. When ājñā cakra is awakened, the higher dimension of consciousness is experienced. For these reasons, sitting in siddhāsana for prolonged periods is considered to bring about the meditative state in itself.

Paścimottānāsana

Paścimottānāsana, back stretching pose, stretches the hamstrings and promotes flexibility in the hip joints. It tones and massages the whole abdominal and pelvic area, and stimulates circulation to the nerves and muscles of the spine. People who have slipped disc or sciatica should not do this practice.

Sukhāsana

Sukhāsana, the easy pose, is the most basic cross-legged posture. Although it is the easiest and most relaxing meditation position for beginners and elderly practitioners, it is difficult to sustain for long periods. In sukhāsana the legs may be crossed in any comfortable manner. Hence, it is not a locked posture, as were the other poses mentioned earlier, and it does not hold the body upright and still for long periods. Furthermore, the knees and thighs may not be directly on the floor, which is an important attribute of the classical meditation postures. When the knees and thighs remain above the floor, the whole body weight is supported by the buttocks, which causes backache to develop. When the knees and thighs rest firmly on the floor, there is a larger and steadier area of support.

Verses 53 to 55: Prāṇāyāma

यमैश्च नियमैश्चैव आसनैश्च सुसंयतः ।
नाडीशुद्धिं च कृत्वादौ प्राणायामं समाचरेत् ।।५३।।
देहमानं स्वाङ्गुलिभिः षण्णवत्यङ्गुलायतम् ।
प्राणः शरीरादधिको द्वादशाङ्गुलमानतः ।।५४।।
देहस्थमनिलं देहसमुद्भूतेन वह्निना ।
न्यूनं समं वा योगेन कुर्वन्ब्रह्विदिष्यते ।।५५।।

yamaiśca niyamaiśca āsanaiśca susaṃyataḥ
nāḍīśuddhiṃ ca kṛtvādau prāṇāyāmaṃ samācaret (53)
dehamānaṃ svāṅgulibhiḥ ṣaṇṇavatyaṅgulāyatam prāṇaḥ
śarīrādadhiko dvādaśāṅgulamānataḥ (54)
dehasthamanilaṃ dehasamudbhūtena vahninā
nyūnaṃ samaṃ vā yogena kurvanbrahvidiṣyate (55)

Vocabulary
ādau: first; *ca*: and; *susaṃyataḥ*: good control; *yamaiḥ-ca niyamaiḥ-ca āsanaiḥ*: of the yamas and niyamas and āsanas; *kṛtvā nāḍī-śuddhiṃ*: having begun purification of the nāḍīs; *samācaretprāṇāyāmam*: one should practise *prāṇāyāma*; *deha-mānam*: height of the body; *ṣaṇṇavati-aṅgula-āyatam*:: ninety-six fingers long; *sva-aṅgulibhiḥ*: by one's own fingers; *prāṇaḥ*: prāṇa; *ānataḥ*: extends; *adhikaḥ*: more than; *dvādaśa-aṅgulam*: twelve fingers; *śarīrāt*: from the body; *kurvan*: making; *anilam*: wind; *dehastham*: located in the body; *nyūnam*: less; *vā samam*: or equal to; *vahninā*: fire; *deha-samudbhūtena*: produced in the body; *yogena*: through yoga; *brahvid-iṣyate*: one gains knowledge of Brahma.

Translation
Having first [gained] good control by means of the yamas, niyamas and āsanas and begun purification of the nāḍīs, one should practise *prāṇāyāma*. The height of the [human] body [is] ninety-six fingers long [when measured]

by one's own fingers. The prāṇa extends more than twelve fingers from the body. Making the wind located in the body less or equal to the fire produced in the body through yoga, one gains knowledge of Brahman.

Commentary

When all spiritual practice is based on the strong foundation of yama and niyama, there is endless joy, peace and ecstasy, as it takes us back to our true nature. We know this intuitively as their opposites cause suffering and turbulence in the mind. The practice of yama removes mental disturbance and dissipation, caused by negative interactions within the world. In order to progress in meditation, the mind must be free from these impurities and at peace within itself.

Mastery of āsana gives flexibility, sensitivity and control over the physical body. It activates and rebalances the prāṇas, energies sustaining the body, and purifies, steadies and focuses the mind. Āsana should always be practised before prāṇāyāma. Prāṇāyāma, meaning 'expansion of vital energy', includes methods using the breath to control the flow of vital energies. Regular practice of prāṇāyāma, eliminates toxins from the nāḍīs, enabling the vital energy to flow freely. Nāḍīs are the subtle channels in or along which the life force, pranic energy, circulates. The main practice in this text is *nāḍī śodhana*, alternate nostril breathing (see Verses 95 to 101).

The pranic body, also known as the subtle body, gives energy, life and movement to the physical body with its many organs and systems. It is described as ninety-six aṅgulas, digits or finger widths, which may amount to about seven to eight feet (210 to 240cm). It is permeates the physical body, and should extend more than twelve finger widths beyond it. In yoga, the subtle, or pranic, body is considered to be very important, as all the practices work on it in various ways to rebalance and awaken it.

Verses 56 to 57: Region of Fire

देहमध्ये शिखिस्थानं तप्तजाम्बूनदप्रभम् ।
त्रिकोणं द्विपदामन्यच्चतुरस्त्रं चतुष्पदम् ।।५६।।
वृत्तं विहङ्गमानां तु सदस्त्रं सर्पजन्मनाम् ।
अष्टास्त्रं स्वेदजानां तु तस्मिन्दीपवदुज्ज्वलम् ।।५७।।

dehamadhye śikhisthānaṃ
taptajāmbūnadaprabham trikoṇaṃ
dvipadāmanyaccaturastraṃ catuṣpadam (56)
vṛttaṃ vihaṅgamānāṃ tu ṣaḍastraṃ
sarpajanmanām aṣṭāstraṃ svedajānāṃ tu
tasmindīpavadujjvalam (57)

Vocabulary

śikhi-sthānam: region of fire; *trikoṇam*: triangular; *prabham*: radiant; *tapta-jāmbūnada*: molten gold; *deha-madhye*: middle of the body; *dvipadām*: two-footed; *catuṣpadām*: in four-footed; *caturaśram*: quadrangular; *vihaṅgānām*: in birds; *vṛttākāram*: round; *ṣaḍastram*: hexagonal; *sarpajanmanām*: in snakes; *aṣṭāstram*: octagonal; *svedajānām*: in those produced by sweat.

Translation

The region of fire, [which is] triangular [and as] radiant [as] molten gold, [is] in the middle of the two-footed [being]. In four-footed [beings], [it is] quadrangular. In birds [it is] round, hexagonal in snakes [and] octagonal in those produced by sweat.

Commentary

At the centre of this field is the *śikhisthāna*, the place of fire. In yoga, we also refer to this centre as the *agni maṇḍala*, and it too plays an important role in the awakening of the subtle energies. In its centre is situated the auspicious, subtle, purifying flame. It is present in all animal species. In humans it is triangular and in the centre of the body, which is two digits above the anus and two digits below the sexual organ. In four-footed animals, it is quadrangular and in the centre of the heart. In birds it is round and in the centre of the abdomen.It is hexagonal in snakes. ‘Those produced by sweat’ are insects, microbes and bacteria.

Verses 58 to 62: Place of the Jīva

कन्दस्थानं मनुष्याणां देहमध्यं नवाङ्गुलम् ।
चतुरङ्गुलमुत्सेधं चतुरङ्गुलमायतम् ।।५८।।
अण्डाकृति तिरश्चां च द्विजानां च चतुष्पदाम् ।
तुन्दमध्यं तदिष्टं वै तन्मध्यं नाभिरिष्यते ।।५९।।
तत्र चक्रं द्वादशारं तेषु विष्णवादिमूर्तयः ।
अहं तत्र स्थितश्चक्रं भ्रामयामि स्वमायया ।।६०।
अरेषु भ्रमते जीवः क्रमेण द्विजसत्तम ।
तन्तुपञ्चरमध्यस्था यथा भ्रमति लूतिका ।।६१।।
प्राणाविरूढश्चरति जीवस्तेन विना न हि
तस्योर्ध्वे कुण्डलीस्थानं नाभिस्तिर्यकथोर्ध्वतः ।।६२।।

kandasthānaṃ manuṣyāṇāṃ dehamadhyaṃ
navāṅgulam caturaṅgulamutsedhaṃ
caturaṅgulamāyatam (58)
aṇḍākṛti tiraścāṃ ca dvijānāṃ ca catuṣpadām
tundamadhyaṃ tadiṣṭaṃ vai tanmadhyaṃ nābhiriṣyate (59)
tatra cakraṃ dvādaśāraṃ teṣu viṣṇavādimūrtayaḥ
ahaṃtatra sthitaścakraṃ bhrāmayāmi svamāyayā (60)
areṣu bhramate jīvaḥ krameṇa dvijasattama
tantupañcaramadhyasthā yathā bhramati lūtikā (61)
prāṇāvirūdhaścarati jīvastena vinā na hi
tasyordhve kuṇḍalīsthānaṃ nābhistiryagathordhvataḥ (62)

Vocabulary

kanda-sthānam: place of the *kanda*; *nava-aṅgulam*: nine digits; *deha-madhyam*: centre of the body; *ujjvalam*: luminous; *dīpavat*: as a lamp; *catuḥ-aṅgulam*: four digits; *utsedham*: in length; *catuḥ-aṅgulam*: four digits; *āyatam*: in width; *iṣṭam aṇḍākṛti*: is oval-shaped; *ca dvijānāṃ ca catuṣpadām*: in both those with two and those with four legs; *ca tiraḥ*: and across; *tunda-madhyam*: middle of the navel; *vai*: indeed; *nābhiḥ*: navel; *iṣyate*: is considered; *tat-madhyam*: its centre; *tatra*: there; *cakram*: cakra; *dvādaśa-āram*: twelve spokes; *teṣu*: in them; *mūrtayaḥ*: deities; *viṣṇau-ādi*: Viṣṇu and others; *aham bhrāmayāmi*: I cause to move about; *sva-māyayā*: through my own power; *cakram*: cakra; *sthitaḥ tatra*: located there; *jīvaḥ*: *jīva*, individual soul; *bhramate*: wanders; *areṣu*: in its spokes; *dvija-sattama*: o excellent Brāhmaṇa; *krameṇa yathā*: in the same way as; *lūtikā*: spider; *bhramati*: wanders about; *madhyasthā*: in the midst of; *pañcāra tantu*: five-spoked cobweb; *jīvaḥ carati*: jīva moves; *prāṇa-avirūdhaḥ*: flowing prāṇa; *vinā tena*: without which; *na hi*: it cannot; *atha*: now; *ūrdhve*: over; *kuṇḍalī-sthānam*: place of the kuṇḍalinī; *tiryak*:; horizontally; *ūrdhvataḥ*: above; *nābhiḥ*: navel.

Translation

The place of the *kanda* is nine digits in the centre of the human body, [and is] luminous as a lamp. [It is] four digits in height [and] four digits in width. It is oval-shaped in both those with two and those with four legs, and across the middle of the navel. Indeed the navel is considered [to be] its centre. There is a cakra with twelve spokes. In them are the deities of Viṣṇu and others. I, through my own power, cause the cakra located there to move about. The jīva whirls among its spokes, o excellent Brāhmaṇa, in the same way as the spider wanders about in the midst of the five-spoked cobweb. The jīva moves by the flowing prāṇa, without which it cannot [exist]. Now over it is the place of the kuṇḍalinī horizontally above the navel.

Commentary

The oval kanda is the root of the three main nāḍīs, or energy channels, *iḍā*, *piṅgalā* and *suṣumnā*, where they unite and separate. The cakra referred to is *maṇipura*, described as having twelve spokes, although usually it is considered to have ten. The deities in maṇipura are Viṣṇu, also called Agni, and the benevolent goddess Lākinī.

Verses 5b to 7 in *Śāṇḍilya Upaniṣad* also say: 'Nine digits [from] the centre of the body [and] four digits [in] width and length [is] an oval. In its middle [is] the navel. There [is] a cakra with twelve spokes, and in its midst the *jīva* wanders, impelled by its good and bad [actions], just as a spider wanders among the threads of a web, so that prāṇa roams about there. In this body, the jīva is carried by prāṇa.'

Remember that the Brāhmaṇa has gone to the world of the Sun and asked the fundamental questions of existence. Here Āditya, the sun god, says 'I, through my own power cause the cakra to move about', because he is the vital cosmic energy behind all matter.

The *Śāṇḍilya* verse says the jīva wanders about 'impelled by its good and bad [actions]', meaning that here the individual self is subject to the karmas of present and past lives. The jīva is trapped in this web of prāṇas, until the kuṇḍalinī awakens, and the jīva travels up to the higher cakras, where it identifies with the ātman, the universal Self.

Verses 63 to 65: Kuṇḍalinī

अष्टप्रकृतिरूपा सा चाष्टधा कुण्डलीकृता ।

यथावद्वायुसारं च ज्वलनादि च नित्यशः ॥६३॥

परितः कन्दपार्श्वे तु निरुध्यैव सदा स्थिता ।

मुखेनैव समावेष्ट्य ब्रह्मरन्ध्रमुखं तथा ॥६४॥

योगकालेन मरुता साग्निना बोधिता सती ।

स्फुरिता हृदयाकाशे नागरूपा महोज्ज्वला ॥६५॥

aṣṭaprakṛtirūpā sā cāṣṭadhā kuṇḍalīkṛtā
yathāvadvāyusāraṃ ca jvalanādi ca nityaśaḥ (63)
paritaḥ kandapārśve tu nirudhyaiva sadā sthitā
mukhenaiva samāveṣṭya brahmarandramukhaṃ tathā (64)
yogakālena marutā sāgninā bodhitā satī
sphuritā hṛdayākāśe nāgarūpā mahojjvalā (65)

Vocabulary

sā: she; *rūpā*: form; *aṣṭa-prakṛti*: eight elements of nature; *ca*: and; *kṛtā*: making; *aṣṭadhā kuṇḍalīḥ*: eightfold coils; *yathāvad*: which; *nityaśaḥ*: constantly; *nirudhya*: having controlled; *ca vāyu-sāram*: both the energy of the vital air; *jvala-nādi*: and the roaring of the fire; *paritaḥ*: all around; *kanda-pārśve*: beside the *kanda*; *sthitā*: she remains; *sadā*: ever; *tathā*: thus; *samāveṣṭya*: covering; *mukhena*: with her mouth; *mukham*: mouth; *yoga-kālena*: at the time of yoga; *sā bodhitā satī*: she is illuminated; *marutā*: by air; *agninā*: by fire; *mahot-jvalā*: great blaze; *nāga-rūpā*: in the form of the serpent; *sphuritā*: breaks forth; *hṛdaya-akāśe*: in the heart space.

Translation

She [kuṇḍalinī has] the form [of] the eight elements of nature, and making eightfold coils, which having constantly controlled both the energy of the vital air and the roaring of the fire all around {and] beside the *kanda*, she remains ever thus, covering with her mouth the mouth of the *brahmarandhra*.At the time of yoga, [when] she is illuminated by air [and] fire, a great blaze in the form of the serpent breaks forth in the heart space.

Commentary

Kuṇḍalinī is the power of Consciousness (*cit-śakti*). Its literal meaning is 'she who is coiled'. Kuṇḍalinī śakti therefore is known as the serpent power, containing the potential divine or infinite energy of the cosmos, pure consciousness. The kuṇḍalinī energy residing at the kanda is in a more dynamic state, ready to awaken and ascend. When she is awakened at maṇipura cakra, she will ascend to the higher cakras and not fall down again to mūlādhāra or *swādhiṣṭhāna*.

The kuṇḍalinī has the form of the eight elements of nature, which she deposits at the cakras on her descent through the suṣumnā. First she deposits the three elements of mind: *buddhi* (intellect), *citta* (memory) and *ahaṃkāra* (ego), at ājñā cakra, at the top of the spinal column. Next she descends to *viśuddhi cakra*, behind the throat, and deposits the element of space. Then she descends to anāhata cakra, behind the heart, and deposits the element of air. Next she descends to maṇipura cakra, behind the navel, and deposits the element of fire. She continues on her journey down to swādhiṣṭhāna cakra, behind the pubis, and deposits the energy of water, and finally she descends to mūlādhāra cakra, above the perineum, and deposits the energy of earth.

These five elements: earth, water, fire, air and space, along with the three elements of mind: buddhi, citta and ahaṃkāra, make eight elements of nature, which all human beings are comprised of. These eight elements represent the evolution of the kuṇḍalinī energy from divine to material, which is the cause of creation. Having assumed the earthly form through the combination and permutation of these elements, one must constantly consume food and water, and breathe air.

The continuous intake of these earthly elements blocks the *brahmarandhra*, the opening of the brahma nāḍī at the fontanelle, holding the spirit in the body, in the same way that the kuṇḍalinī blocks the opening of suṣumnā at the lower centres with her own mouth at the kanda.

The 'energy of vital air' refers to *samāna*, which moves from side to side, stimulating digestion. When yoga practices are performed, *prāṇa*, the upward vital air, and *apāna*, the downward vital air, come together at the navel centre, *maṇipura kṣetram*, creating a powerful hot energy, awakening maṇipura cakra, and shooting up to anāhata cakra, where the aspiring yogi lives in universal wisdom.[20]

Verses 66 to 69: Centre of the Body

अपानाद्द्व्यङ्गुलादूर्ध्वमधो मेढ्रस्य तावता ।
देहमध्यं मनुष्याणां हृन्मध्यं तु चतुष्पदाम् ॥६६॥
इतरेषां तुन्दमध्ये नानानाडीसमावृतम् ।
चतुष्प्रकारद्व्ययुते देहमध्ये सुषुम्नया ॥६७॥
कन्दमध्ये स्थिता नाडी सुषुम्ना सुप्रतिष्ठिता ।
पद्मसूत्रप्रतीकाशा ऋजुरूर्ध्वप्रवर्तिती ॥६८॥
ब्रह्मणो विवरं यावद्विद्युदाभामनालकम् ।
वैष्णवी ब्रह्मनाडी च निर्वाणप्राप्तिपद्धतिः ॥६९॥

apānāddvyaṅgulādūrdhvamadho meḍhrasya tāvatā
dehamadhyaṃ manuṣyāṇāṃ hṛnmadhyaṃ tucatuṣpadām(66)
itareṣāṃ tundamadhye nānānāḍīsamāvṛtam
catuṣprakāradvyayute dehamadhye suṣumnayā (67)
kandamadhye sthitā nāḍī suṣumnā supratiṣṭhitā
padmasūtrapratīkāśā ṛjurūrdhvapravartitī (68)
brahmaṇo vivaraṃ yāvadvidyudābhāmanālakam
vaiṣṇavī brahmanāḍī ca nirvāṇaprāptipaddhatiḥ(69)

Vocabulary

dvi-aṅgulāt: two fingers; *ūrdhvam*: upwards; *apānāt*: from apāna; *tāvatā*: to; *adhaḥ*: below; *meḍhrasya*: genital organ; *deha-madhyam*: middle of the body; *manuṣyāṇām*: in humans; *hṛt-madhyam*: heart centre; *catur-padām*: in the four-footed; *itareṣām*: in the rest; *tunda-madhye*: in the centre of the abdomen; *nānā-nāḍī-samāvṛtam*: enveloped by many nāḍīs; *deha-madhye*: in the centre of the body; *catur-prakāra*: four times; *dvi-ayute*: twenty thousand; *suṣumnayā*: with suṣumnā; *sthitā nāḍī suṣumnā*: is suṣumnā nāḍī ; *supratiṣṭhitā*: firmly established; *kanda-madhye*: in the centre of the kanda; *brahmanāḍī*: *brahmanāḍī,* the innermost nāḍī within suṣumnā; *ābhām*: luminous; *vidyut*: lightning; *pravartitī*: moves to; *ṛjuḥ-ūrdhva*: straight upwards;
pratīkāśā: like; *padma-sūtra*: stalk of a lotus; *brahmaṇaḥ vivaram*: brahma opening; *yāvat*: right up to; *anālakam*:

stalkless; *vaiṣṇavī*: divine power of Viṣṇu; *ca paddhatiḥ*: and the way; *nirvāṇa-prāpti*: to reach final liberation.

Translation

Two fingers upwards from apāna [at maṇipura] to [two fingers] below the genital organ [is] the middle of the body in humans. The heart centre [is the middle of the body] in the four-footed. In the rest [it is] in the centre of the abdomen enveloped by many nāḍīs. In the centre of the body [with] the four times twenty thousand nāḍīs is suṣumnā nāḍī firmly established in the centre of the kanda, *Brahmanāḍī*, luminous [as] lightning, moves straight upwards like the stalk of a lotus to the Brahman opening right up to the stalkless divine power of Viṣṇu and the way to reach final liberation.

Commentary

When the energy of apāna is redirected upward, it unites with *agni*, the element of fire, behind the navel. Together the forces of apāna and agni merge with prāṇa at the maṇipura cakra. Having united with prāṇa and apāna, agni, quickly descends to the mūlādhāra cakra, where the kuṇḍalinī lies coiled, fast asleep. Kuṇḍalinī is heated by agni and stirred up by the vāyus, apāna and prāṇa. This causes her to awaken suddenly, and she enters the mouth of suṣumnā, located just above the mūlādhāra cakra. Then she stretches out her coils and begins to ascend the *brahmanāḍī*, the innermost nāḍī within suṣumnā.

The brahmanāḍī can be visualized as a fiery luminous thread, and the kuṇḍalinī as a point of light moving up it. As kuṇḍalinī ascends through the cakras, the limited state of consciousness falls away, and the consciousness assumes its pure, expanded state.

Verses 70 to 76: Eight Nāḍīs

इडा च पिङ्गला चैव तस्याः सव्येतरे स्थिते ।
इडा समुत्थिता कन्दाद्वामनासापुटावधिः ।।७०।।
पिङ्गला चोत्थिता तस्माद्दक्षनासापुटावधिः ।
गान्धारी हस्तिजिह्वा च द्वे चान्ये नाडिके स्थिते ।।७१।।
पुरतः पृष्ठस्तस्य वामेतरदृशौ प्रति ।
पूषायशस्विनीनाड्यौ तस्मादेव समुत्थिते ।।७२।।
सव्येतरश्रुत्यवधि पायुमूलादलम्बुसा ।
अधोगता शुभा नाडी मेढ्रान्तावधिरायता ।।७३।।
पादाङ्गुष्ठावधिः कन्दादधोयाता च कौशिकी ।
दशप्रकारभूतास्ताः कथिताः कन्दसंभवाः ।।७४।।
तन्मूला बहवो नाड्यः स्थूलसूक्ष्माश्च नाडिकाः ।
द्वासप्ततिसहस्राणि स्थूलाः सूक्ष्माश्च नाड्यः ।।७५।।
संख्यातुं नैव शक्यन्ते स्थूलमूलाः ।
यथाश्वत्थदले सूक्ष्मा स्थूलाश्च विततास्तथा ।।७६।।

iḍā ca piṅgalā caiva tasyāḥ savyetare sthite
iḍā samutthitā kandādvāmanāsāpuṭāvadhiḥ (70)
piṅgalā cotthitā tasmāddakṣanāsāpuṭāvadhiḥ
gāndhārī hastijihvā ca dve cānye nāḍike sthite (71)
purataḥ pṛṣṭhastasya vāmetaradṛśau prati
pūṣāyaśasvinīnāḍyau tasmādeva samutthite (72)
savyetaraśrutyavadhi pāyumūlādalambusā
adhogatā śubhā nāḍī meḍhrāntāvadhirāyatā (73)
pādāṅguṣṭhāvadhiḥ kandādadhoyātā ca kauśikī
daśaprakārabhūtāstāḥ kathitāḥ kandasaṃbhavāḥ (74)
tanmūlā bahavo nāḍyaḥ sthūlasūkṣmāśca nāḍikāḥ
dvāsaptatisahasrāṇi sthūlāḥ sūkṣmāśca nāḍyaḥ (75)
saṃkhyātuṃ naiva śakyante sthūlamūlāḥ
yathāśvatthadale sūkṣmā sthūlāśca vitatāstathā (76)

Vocabulary

iḍā ca piṅgalā: *iḍā* and *piṅgalā*; *sthite*: are; *tasyāḥ*: its; *savyetare*: left and right; *iḍā samutthitā*: iḍā rises; *kandāt*: from the kanda; *puṭa-avadhiḥ*: right up to the cavity; *vām-anāsā*: left nostril; *ca piṅgalā utthitā*: and piṅgalā extends; *tasmāt*: from it; *puṭa-avadhiḥ*: right up to the cavity; *dakṣa-nāsā*: right nostril; *ca gāndhārī ca hastijihvā*: both *gāndhārī* and *hastijihvā*; *sthite*: are; *dve anye nāḍike*: two other nāḍīs; *tasya*: at its; *purataḥ*: front; *pṛṣṭhaḥ*: back; *prati*: up to; *dṛśau*: both eyes; *pūṣā-yaśasvinīnāḍyau*: *pūṣā* and *yaśasvinī* nāḍīs; *samutthite*: rise; *avadhi*: up to; *savyetara śruti*: left and right ears; *pāyu-mūlāt*: from the base of the anus; *śubhā nāḍī*: auspicious nāḍī; *adhogatā*: goes down; *āyatā*: extends; *anta-avadhiḥ*: right to the end of; *meḍhra*: penis; *kauśikī adhoyātā*: goes down; *kandāt*: from the kanda; *pādāṅguṣṭha-avadhiḥ*: right to the big toe; *tāḥ*: these; *daśa-prakāra*: ten types; *bhūtāḥ*: channels; *kathitāḥ*: are said to; *kanda-saṃbhavāḥ*: originate from the kanda; *tat-mūlā*: from that root; *bahavaḥ*: many; *sthūla-sūkṣmāḥ nāḍyaḥ*: gross and subtle nāḍīs; *dvāsaptati-sahasrāṇi*: seventy-two thousand; *sthūlāḥ ca sūkṣmāḥ nāḍyaḥ*: gross and subtle nāḍīs; *sthūla-mūlāḥ*: subtle roots; *na-eva śakyante*: cannot even; *saṃkhyātum*: be counted; *yathā*: just as; *sūkṣmā ca sthūlāḥ dale*: small and large leaves; *aśvattha*: holy fig tree; *vitatāḥ*: spread far beyond.

Translation

Iḍā and piṅgalā [nāḍīs] are on its left and right. Iḍā rises from the kanda right up to the cavity [of] the left nostril, and piṅgalā extends from it right up to the cavity [of] the right nostril. Both *gāndhārī* and *hastijihvā* are two other nāḍīs. [They are] at its front [and] back up to both eyes. The *pūṣā* and *yaśasvinī* nāḍīs rise up to the left and right ears from the base of the anus. *Alambusā*, the auspicious nāḍī, goes down [and] extends right to the end of the penis. *Kauśikī* goes down from the kanda right to the big toe. These ten types of channels are said to originate from the kanda.

From that root [are] many gross and subtle nāḍīs. [There are] seventy-two thousand gross and subtle nāḍīs. The subtle roots cannot even be counted, just as the small and large leaves [of] the holy fig tree spread far beyond.

Commentary

Here are listed eight main nāḍīs which originate at the kanda. Of these, the two major ones are iḍā and piṅgalā. When *mahāprāṇa* (unmanifest cosmic energy) and *prakṛti* (manifest cosmic energy) combine, this is known as prāṇa. From this prāṇa come iḍā and piṅgalā. Iḍā rises from the kanda through the cakras on the left side of the body up to ājñā cakra, and is the passive, mental or lunar force. It is also called *cit śakti*. It controls our mental experiences and the four organs of the mind (buddhi, manas, citta and ahaṃkāra), as well as manomaya koṣa and vijñānamaya koṣa. Piṅgalā rises from the kanda through the cakras on the right side of the body, and is the dynamic or solar force. It is also called *prāṇa śakti*. It controls physical energy, including stamina, stimulation, relaxation and tension as well as annamaya and ānandamaya koṣas.

The other eight nāḍīs mentioned also originate at the kanda, the life force (prāṇa) flowing upwards, as they pass through each cakra. The description of the ten major nāḍīs is found in several upaniṣads and classical texts, such as the *Śiva Swarodaya*. The yogis and rishis of old had originally seen these channels during their meditation, and later described what they had seen to their devotees and disciples. 'Just as the leaf of the holy fig tree is pervaded with veins, so the body is pervaded with nāḍīs.' [21]

Verses 77 to 82: Ten Vital Airs

प्राणापानौ समानश्च उदानो व्यान एव च ।
नागः कूर्मश्च कृकरो देवदत्तो धनंजयः ।।७७।।
चरन्ति दशनाडीषु दश प्रानादिवायवः ।
प्रानादिपञ्चकं तेषु प्रधानं तत्र च द्वयम् ।।७८।।
प्राण एवाथवा ज्येष्ठो जीवात्मानं बिभर्ति यः ।
आस्यनासिकयोर्मध्यं हृदयं नाभिमण्डलम् ।।७९।।
पादाङ्गुष्ठमिति प्राणस्थानानि द्विजसत्तम् ।
अपानश्चरति ब्रह्मन्गुदमेढ्रोरुजानुषु ।।८०।।
समानः सर्वगात्रेषु सर्वव्यापी व्यवस्थितः ।
उदानः सर्वसन्धिस्थः पादयोर्हस्तयोरपि ।।८१।।
व्यानः श्रोत्रोरुकट्यां च गुल्फस्कन्धगलेषु च ।
नागादिवायवः पञ्च त्वगस्थ्यादिषु संस्थिताः ।।८२।।

prāṇāpānau. samānaśca udāno vyāna eva ca
nāgaḥ kūrmaśca kṛkaro devadatto dhanaṃjayaḥ (77)
caranti daśanāḍīṣu daśa prāṇādivāyavaḥ
prāṇādipañcakaṃ teṣu pradhānaṃ tatra ca dvayam (78)
prāṇa evāthavā jyeṣṭho jīvātmānaṃ bibharti yaḥ
āsyanāsikayormadhyaṃ hṛdayaṃ nābhimaṇḍalam (79)
pādāṅguṣṭhamiti prāṇasthānāni dvijasattam
apānaścarati brahmangudameḍhrorujānuṣu (80)
samānaḥ sarvagātreṣu sarvavyāpī vyavasthitaḥ
udānaḥ sarvasandhisthaḥ pādayorhastayorapi (81)
vyānaḥ śrotrorukaṭyāṃ ca gulphaskandhagaleṣu ca
nāgādivāyavaḥ pañca tvagasthyādiṣu saṃsthitāḥ (82)

Vocabulary

daśa vāyavaḥ: ten vital airs; *prāṇa-ādi*: beginning with prāṇa; *eva ca*: and also; *caranti*: move about; *daśa-nāḍīṣu*: in ten nāḍīs; *prāṇa-ādi-pañcakam*: first five prāṇas; *pradhānam*: major; *ca teṣu*: of those; *jyeṣṭhaḥ dvayam prāṇaḥ*: first two prāṇas; *yaḥ iti*: which it is said; *bibharti*:

support; *jīvātmānam*: individual soul; *āsya-nāsikayoḥ-madhyam*: centre of the mouth and nose; *hṛdayam*: heart; *nābhi-maṇḍalam*: navel; *pāda-aṅguṣṭham*: big toes; *prāṇa-sthānāni*: abodes of prāṇa; *dvija-sattam*: o Excellent Brāhmaṇa; *apānaḥ-carati*: apāna moves: *guda-meḍhra-ūru-jānuṣu*: in the anus, genitals, thighs and knees; *brahman*: o Brāhmaṇa; *samānaḥ sarva-vyāpī*: samāna spreads throughout; *sarva-gātreṣu*: all the limbs; *udānaḥ vyavasthitaḥ*: udāna is located in; *sarva-sandhisthaḥ*: all the joints; *pādayoḥ-hastayoḥ*: of feet and hands; *api*: too; *vyānaḥ śrotra-ūru-kaṭyām*: vyāna is in the ears, hips and waist; *ca gulpha-skandha-galeṣu*: and in the ankles, shoulders and neck; *pañca*: five; *nāga-ādi-vāyavaḥ*: five winds of nāga and others; *saṃsthitāḥ*: are located; *tvag-asthi-ādiṣu*: in the skin and bones etc.

Translation

The ten vital airs, beginning with prāṇa, [are] *prāṇa apāna samāna, udāna, vyāna*, and also *nāga, kūrma, kṛkara*, *devadatta* and *dhanaṃjaya* move about in ten nāḍīs. The first five [are] the major [ones] in these [nāḍīs] and of those the first two prāṇas [are those], which it is said, support the individual soul. The centre of the mouth and nose, the heart, navel [and] big toes are the abodes of prāṇa, o Excellent Twice-born one! Apāna moves in the anus, genitals, thighs and knees, o Brāhmaṇa! Samāna spreads throughout all the limbs. Udāna is located in all the joints of feet and hands too. Vyāna is in the ears, hips and waist, and in the ankles, shoulders and neck. The five winds of Nāga and others are located in the skin and bones etc.

Commentary

These verses name the five major and five minor prāṇas. The five major prāṇas are: *prāṇa, apāna, vyāna, samāna*, and *udāna*. These five prāṇas continuously sustain the physical body with vitality and life. Of these five, prāṇa is considered to be the most important. It flows upward from the navel to the heart and in the nostrils. It supports the lungs and heart. Vyāna flows in the region of the shoulders, neck and head, sustaining the sensory organs, such as ears, eyes, nose, tongue, as well as the nervous system and the brain. Apāna flows downward from the navel to the anus, hips, thighs and knees. It sustains the reproductive and excretory organs. Udāna flows in the hands and feet. Samāna flows throughout the whole body. The five minor prāṇas, beginning with Nāga, are said to be located in the skin and bones.

The locations given here may differ to those given in other classical texts. The *Śiva Swarodaya*, says that prāṇa is at the heart, samāna at the navel region, udāna at the throat, and vyāna pervades the whole body.

Verses 83 to 89a: Functions of the Vital Airs

तुन्दस्थजलमन्नं च तसादीनि समीकृतम् ।
तुन्दमध्यगतः प्राणस्तानि कुर्यात्पृथक्पृथक् ।।८३।।
इत्यादिचेष्टनं प्राणः करोति च पृथक् स्थितम्
अपानवायुर्मूत्रादेः करोति च विसर्जनम् ।।८४।।
प्राणापानादिचेष्टादि क्रियते व्यानवायुना ।
उज्जीर्यते शरीरस्थमुदानेन नभस्वता ।।८५।।
पोषणादिशरीरस्य समानः कुरुते सदा ।
उद्गारादिक्रियो नागः कूर्मोऽक्षादिनिमीलनः ।।८६।।
कृकरः क्षुधयोः कर्ता दत्तो निद्रादिकर्मकृत् ।
कृतगात्रस्य शोभादेर्धनंजय उदाहृतः ।।८७।।
नाडीभेदं मरुद्भेदं मरुतां स्थानमेव च ।
चेष्टाश्च विविधास्तेषां ज्ञात्वैव द्विजसत्तम् ।।८८।।
शुद्धौ यतेत नाडीनां पूर्वोक्तज्ञानसंयुतः ।८९।

tundasthajalamannaṃ ca rasādīni samīkṛtam
tundamadhyagataḥ prāṇastāni kuryātpṛthakpṛthak (83)
ityādiceṣṭanaṃ prāṇaḥ karoti ca pṛthak sthitam
apānavāyurmūtrādeḥ karoti ca visarjanam (84)
prāṇāpānādiceṣṭādi kriyate vyānavāyunā
ujjīryate śarīrasthamudānena nabhasvatā (85)
poṣaṇādiśarīrasya samānaḥ kurute sadā
udgārādikriyo nāgaḥ kūrmo'kṣādinimīlanaḥ (86)
kṛkaraḥ kṣudhayoḥ kartā datto nidrādikarmakṛt
kṛtagātrasya śobhāderdhanaṃjaya udāhṛtaḥ (87)
nāḍībhedaṃ marudbhedaṃ marutāṃ sthānameva ca
ceṣṭāśca vividhāsteṣāṃ jñātvaiva dvijasattam (88)
śuddhau yateta nāḍīnāṃ pūrvoktajñānasaṃyutaḥ (89a)

Vocabulary

jalam-annam: water, food; *ca rasa-ādīni*: and fluids etc; *tunda-stha*: in the belly; *samīkṛtam*: are assimilated; *prāṇaḥ*: prāṇa; *gataḥ*: having gone to; *tunda-madhya*: centre of the belly; *kuryāt-pṛthak tāni*: separates them; *pṛthak*: from each other; *iti*: thus; *prāṇaḥ karoti ceṣṭanam ādi*: prāṇa performs these; *sthitam*: remaining; *pṛthak*: separate; *apāna-vāyuḥ*: apāna wind; *karoti visarjanam*: discharges; *mūtra-ādeḥ*: urine etc; *ceṣṭā-ādi*: actions; *prāṇa-apāna-ādi*: prāṇa and apāna etc; *kriyate*: is made; *vyāna-vāyunā*: by the vyāna wind; *ujjīryate*: stimulated; *udānena nabhasvatā*: by the udāna wind; *śarīra-stham*: in the body; *samānaḥ sadā*: samānaḥ always; *kurute*: performs; *poṣaṇa-ādi*: nourishing etc; *śarīrasya*: of the body; *kriyaḥ nāgaḥ*: action of nāga; *udgāra-ādi*: belching etc; *kūrmaḥ nimīlanaḥ akṣa-ādi*: kūrma [is] shutting the eyes etc; *kṛkaraḥ kartā*: kṛkara is the cause; *kṣudhayoḥ*: of hunger; *dattaḥ karmakṛt*: devadatta controls; *nidrā-ādi*: sleep etc; *dhanaṃjaya udāhṛtaḥ*: dhanaṃjaya is said to; *kṛta śobhādeḥ*: bring lustre; *gātrasya*: to the body; *jñātva-eva*: having thus known; *dvijasattam*: o Brāhmaṇa; *nāḍī-bhedam*: different nāḍīs; *ca marud-bhedam*: and the different vital airs; *sthānam*: position; *marutām*: of the vital airs; *ca teṣām*: and their; *vividhāḥ ceṣṭāḥ*: diverse functions; *jñāna-saṃyutaḥ*: absorbed knowledge; *pūrva-ukta*: mentioned above; *yateta*: one should do; *śuddhau*: purification; *nāḍīnām*: of the nāḍīs.

Translation

The water, food and other fluids in the belly are assimilated, [and] prāṇa, having gone to the centre of the belly, separates them from each other. Thus the prāṇa performs these [functions], remaining separate. The apāna wind discharges urine etc. The actions of prāṇa and apāna etc are made by the vyāna wind and stimulated by the udāna wind in the body. Samāna always performs the nourishing etc of the body. The action [of] nāga [is] belching etc, [and of] kūrma [is] shutting the eyes etc. Kṛkara causes hunger, devadatta controls sleep etc [and] dhanaṃjaya is said to bring lustre to the body. Having thus known, o Brāhmaṇa, the differences among the various nāḍīs and vital airs, [and] the position of the vital airs and their diverse functions, and absorbed the knowledge mentioned above, one should do purification of the nāḍīs.

Commentary

Prāṇa and apāna stimulate the digestive process around maṇipura cakra in the small intestine, the main organ of digestion. Prāṇa is also the energy responsible for sighing, coughing and exhalation Apāna is responsible for evacuation of faeces, urine, gas and wind, and the foetus at the time of birth. Samāna vitalises the entire body. Udāna flows upward and mobilises the hands and feet. Vyāna flows in the region of the shoulders, neck and head, and vitalises the senses and brain.

Of the five minor prāṇas, nāga is responsible for belching, vomiting and hiccupping, thus relieving pressure on the abdomen. Kūrma causes blinking and shutting of the eyes, 'thus regulating the intensity of light by controlling the size of the iris. The eyes are the index of the brain. Any movement in the brain is reflected in the eyes. By stilling the eyes, i.e., by control of kūrma-vāyu, one can still one's thoughts and make one's brain immobile.'[22] Kṛkara causes hunger and devadatta is the cause of yawning, inducing sleep. Dhanaṃjaya produces phlegm and gives lustre to the body, which remains even after death.[23]

Once one has a good understanding of the cakras, prāṇas and nāḍīs of the subtle or pranic body and their functions, one can do the practices of purifying the nāḍīs.

Verses 89b to 91: Place of Sādhana

विविक्तदेशमासाद्य सर्वसंबन्धवर्जितः ।।८९।।
योगाङ्गद्रव्यसंपूर्णं तत्र दारुमये शुभे ।
आसने कल्पिते दर्भकुशकृष्णाजिनादिभिः ।।९०।।
तावदासनमुत्सेधे तावद्द्वयसमायते ।
उपविश्यासनं सम्यक्स्वस्तिकादि यथारुचि ।।९१।।

viviktadeśamāsādya sarvasaṃbandhavarjitaḥ (89b)
yogāṅgadravyasaṃpūrṇaṃ tatra dārumaye śubhe
āsane kalpite darbhakuśakṛṣṇājinādibhiḥ (90)
tāvadāsanamutsedhe tāvaddvayasamāyate
upaviśyāsanaṃ samyaksvastikādi yathāruci (91)

Vocabulary

āsādya: having settled in; *vivikta-deśam*: secluded place; *varjitaḥ*: renounced; *sarva-saṃbandha*: all associations; *tatra*: there; *saṃpūrṇam*: having acquired; *dravya*: materials; *yoga-āṅga*: practice of yoga; *kalpite*: one should make; *śubhe*: comfortable; *dārumaye*: wooden; *āsane*: seat; *darbha-kuśa-kṛṣṇa-ajina-ādibhiḥ*: with *darbha kuśa* and black deerskin etc; *upaviśi-āsanam*: sit in āsana; *samyak*: correctly; *yathāruci*: of one's choice; *svastika-ādi*: *svastikāsana* etc; *āsanam-utsedhe*: in an upright posture; *tāvat* . . . *tāvat*: both . . . and . . . *dvayasamāyate*: extended.

Translation

Having settled in a secluded place, renounced all associations, and, having acquired materials there [for] the practice of yoga, one should make a comfortable wooden seat with *darbha kuśa* and black deerskin etc. [and] sit correctly in the āsana of one's choice, such as svastikāsana etc, both in an upright and extended posture.

Commentary

Once the aspirant has practised the yamas and niyamas sincerely and diligently to clear the mind and has avoided outside influences, he should find a peaceful solitary place in nature to meditate, which has all the basic needs of fresh food and water. He should make himself a meditation hut, suitable for one person, with a door, and smeared with cow dung for insulation.[24]

After preparing the space for sādhana, the practitioner then prepares the seat. The traditional seat for the practice of yoga was very specific and also scientific. The seat should be of medium height, not too high and not too low. This means there should be a feeling of connection and balance with the earth. This connection may be lost, when the seat is too elevated. At the same time, the seat is to be somewhat elevated for comfort and also to avoid the disturbance of any insect or creature, which may crawl in from outside.

The seat was generally comprised of three layers: a pile of *kuśa* grass on the bottom, covered by a deer skin, and finally a clean cotton cloth placed on the top. Kuśa grass creates a cushion for the buttocks and hips, and is also an excellent energy conductor. The deer skin has auspicious properties for yoga, as the deer is known to be gentle, non-violent, alert and fleet. The cotton cloth placed on the top is again for comfort and also absorption.

Having prepared the seat, the practitioner sits upon it in the position of svastikāsana or any other meditation posture which keeps the body steady and upright. [25]

Verses 92 to 94: Posture for Prāṇāyāma

बद्ध्वा प्रागासनं ऋजुकायः समाहितः ।
नासाग्रयस्तनयनो दन्तैर्दन्तानसंस्पृशन् ।।९२।।
रसनां तालुनि न्यस्य स्वस्थचित्तो निरामयः ।
आकुञ्चितशिरः किंचिन्निबध्नन्योगमुद्रया ।।९३।।
हस्तौ यथोक्तविधिना प्राणायामं समाचरेत् ।
रेचनं पूरणं वायोः शोधनं रेचनं तथा ।।९४।।

baddhvā prāgāsanaṃ ṛjukāyaḥ samāhitaḥ
nāsāgrayastanayano dantairdantānasaṃspṛśan (92)
rasanāṃ tāluni nyasya svasthacitto nirāmayaḥ
ākuñcitaśiraḥ kiṃcinnibadhnanyogamudrayā (93)
hastau yathoktavidhinā prāṇāyāmaṃ samācaret
recanaṃ pūraṇaṃ vāyoḥ śodhanaṃ recanaṃ tathā (94)

Vocabulary

baddhvā āsanam: being fixed in āsana; *prāk*: as before; *ṛju-kāyaḥ*: body erect; *samāhitaḥ*: steady; *nayanaḥ*: gaze; *yasta*: placed at; *nāsāgra*: nosetip; *asaṃspṛśan*: not touching; *dantān*: teeth; *dantaiḥ*: with the teeth; *rasanām*: tongue; *nyasya*: placed; *tāluni*: on the palate; *cittaḥ nirāmayaḥ*: free from thoughts; *svastha*: abiding in the Self; *śiraḥ*: head; *ākuñcita kiṃcit*: inclined slightly; *nibadhnan*: holding; *hastau*: hands; *yoga-mudrayā*: in *yoga mudrā*; *samācaret prāṇāyāmam*: one should practise *prāṇāyāma*; *vidhinā*: by the method; *yathā ukta*: prescribed; *pūraṇam*: inhaling; *recanam*: exhaling; *tathā*: therefore; *recanam*: exhalation; *śodhanam*: purification; *vayoḥ*: of the vital airs.

Translation

Being fixed in āsana as before, the body erect [and] steady, the gaze placed at the nosetip, not touching the teeth with the teeth, the tongue placed on the palate, free from thoughts, abiding in the Self, the head inclined slightly, holding the hands in *yoga mudrā*, one should practise *prāṇāyāma* by the prescribed method, inhaling [and] exhaling. Therefore exhalation [is] purification of the vital airs.

Commentary

The body must be erect and steady and fixed in a recommended seated meditation posture, so that mūlādhāra cakra at the earth element is stimulated and the prāṇa can be directed upwards through the cakras to ājñā and beyond. Nosetip gazing is important as it is a trigger point for mūlādhāra cakra, as the sense of the earth element is smell. Although the body is erect, it should be relaxed, not tense, so that the head leans forward very slightly and the two rows of teeth are a bit apart. The underside of the tongue touching the palate is the mild form of *khecarī mudrā*, which gives stillness, quiet and introversion.

Yoga mudrās help to channel the flow of prāṇa and awaken the dormant spiritual forces. The fingers and palms of the hands are constantly sending prāṇa out into the external environment. The function of meditative mudrās is to redirect the prāṇa into the body. The verse refers to a hand mudrā, such as *jñāna mudrā*, *jñāna* meaning spiritual wisdom and knowledge, *mudrā* meaning subtle gesture or seal, because it controls the prāṇa; or *cin mudrā* which is the same as jñāna mudrā, except that the palms of the hands face upwards and the backs of the hands rest on the knees. In both, the index fingers are bent, the tips resting against the inside base of the thumbs. The other three fingers are stretched out, relaxed and slightly apart. The little finger, ring finger and middle finger represent the *guṇas*, the three qualities of nature inherent in all creation, *tamas* (inertia, stability), *rajas* (activity, creativity) and *sattva* (luminosity, harmony). The index finger represents the individual consciousness, and the thumb the universal or supreme consciousness. The symbolism of these mudrās is the individual (index finger) bowing down to the power of the supreme consciousness (thumb), and the union of the individual consciousness with the supreme consciousness, thus transcending the three guṇas, which is the aim of yoga.

Impurities in the nāḍīs impede the ascent of *kuṇḍalinī śakti* up suṣumnā, whereas their purity facilitates it. This is the work of prāṇāyāma. With each exhalation, toxins are removed, purifying the nāḍīs.

Verses 95 to 101: Nāḍī Śodhana Leads to Kumbhaka

चतुर्भिः क्लेशनं वायोः प्राणायाम उदीर्यते ।
हस्तेन दक्षिणेनैव पीडयेन्नासिकापुटम् ।।९५।।
शनैः शनैरथ बहिहः प्रत्रिपेत्पिङ्गलानिलम् ।
इडया वायुमापूर्य ब्रह्मन्षोडशमात्रया ।।९६।।
पूरितं कुम्भयेत्पश्चाच्चतुःषष्ट्या तु मात्रया ।
द्वात्रिंशन्मात्रया सम्यग्रेचयेत्पिङ्गलानिलम् ।।९७।।
एवं पुनः पुनः कार्यं व्युत्क्रमानुक्रमेण तु
संपूर्णकुम्भवद्देहं कुम्भयेन्मातरिश्चना ।।९८।।
पूरणान्नाड्यः सर्वाः पूर्यन्ते मातरिश्चना ।
एवं कृते सति ब्रह्मंश्चरन्ति दश वायवः ।।९९।।
हृदयाम्भोरुहं चापि व्याकोचं भवति स्फुटम् ।
तत्र पश्येत्परात्मानं वासुदेवमकल्मषम् ।।१००।।
प्रातर्माध्यन्दिने सायमर्धरात्रे च कुम्भकान् ।
शनैरशीतिपर्यन्तं चतुर्वारं समभ्यसेत् ।।१०१।।

caturbhiḥ kleśanaṃ vāyoḥ prāṇāyāma udīryate hastena
dakṣiṇenaiva pīḍayennāsikāpuṭam (95)
śanaiḥ śanairatha bahiḥ pratripetpiṅgalānilam
iḍayā vāyumāpūrya brahmanṣoḍaśamātrayā (96)
pūritaṃ kumbhayetpaścāccatuḥṣaṣṭyā tu mātrayā
dvātriṃśanmātrayā samyagrecayetpiṅgalānilam (97)
evaṃ punaḥ punaḥ kāryaṃ vyutkramānukrameṇa tu
saṃpūrṇakumbhavaddehaṃ kumbhayenmātariścanā (98)
pūraṇānnāḍyaḥ sarvāḥ pūryante mātariścanā
evaṃ kṛte sati brahmaṃścaranti daśa vāyavaḥ (99)
hṛdayāmbhoruhaṃ cāpi vyākocaṃ bhavati sphuṭam
tatra paśyetparātmānaṃ vāsudevamakalmaṣam (100)
prātarmādhyandine sāyamardharātre ca kumbhakān
śanairaśītiparyantaṃ caturvāraṃ samabhyaset (101

Vocabulary

udīryate prāṇāyāmaḥ: it is called *prāṇāyāma*; *caturbhiḥ kleśanam*: through the four activities; *vāyoḥ*: of the breath; *pīḍayet*: one should press; *puṭam*: purified; *nāsikā*: nostril; *dakṣiṇena hastena*: with the right hand; *vāyum-āpūrya*: having inhaled; *iḍayā*: through the left nostril; *ṣoḍaśa-mātrayā*: sixteen *mātrās*; *atha*: now; *śanaiḥ śanaiḥ*: gradually; *bahiḥ anilam pratripet*: one should exhale; *piṅgalā*: right nostril; *brahman*: o Brahman; *paścāt pūritam*: after inhaling; *kumbhayet*: one should retain; *catuḥṣaṣṭyā mātrayā*: sixty-four mātrās; *tu recayet anilam*: then exhale; *piṅgalā*: right nostril; *samyak dvātriṃśat-mātrayā*: exactly thirty-two mātrās; *evam*: thus; *kāryam*: is to be done; *anukrameṇa*: in sequence; *vyut-krama*: in the reverse order; *saṃpūrṇa*: inhaled; *mātariḥ*: wind; *kumbhayet*: is retained; *kumbhavat*: like a pot; *deham*: body.

pūraṇāt: when inflated; *sarvāḥ nāḍyaḥ*: all the nāḍīs; *pūryante*: are filled with; *mātariścanā*: vital wind; *sati kṛte*: when [this] is being done; *evam*: thus; *daśa vāyavaḥ*: ten winds; *caranti*: move about; *hṛdaya-ambhoruham*: lotus heart; *bhavati*: becomes; *vyākocam*: fully expanded; *ca api sphuṭam*: and also clear; *paśyet*: one can see; *tatra*: there; *vāsudevam-akalmaṣam*: pure Vāsudeva; *parātmānam*: Supreme Soul; *samabhyaset*: one should practise; *kumbhakān*: breath retention; *caturvāram*: four times; *prātaḥ*: in the morning; *mādhyandine*: at midday; *sāyam*: in the evening; *ca ardharātre*: and at midnight; *śanaiḥ*: gradually; *aśīti-paryantam*: up to eighty [times].

Translation

It is called prāṇāyāma through the four activities of the breath. One should press the purified nostril with the right hand. Having inhaled through the left nostril sixteen mātrās, one should now gradually exhale through the right nostril, o Brahman. After inhaling one should retain [the breath] for sixty-four mātrās, then exhale through the right nostril for

exactly thirty-two mātrās. Thus [this practice] is to be done in sequence [and] in the reverse order.
The inhaled wind is retained like a pot [in] the body.

O Brahman, when inflated all the nāḍīs are filled with vital wind. When [this] is being done thus, the ten winds move about. The lotus heart becomes fully expanded and also clear. One can see there the pure Vāsudeva [as] the Supreme Soul. One should practise breath retention four times [a day], in the morning, at midday, in the evening and at midnight, gradually up to eighty [times].

Commentary
Prāṇāyāma means expansion of prāṇa by means of the breath. The four activities of the breath are inhalation, inner retention, exhalation and external retention.

Iḍā is the flow of lunar or mental energy, which passes through the left nostril. Piṅgalā is the flow of solar or vital energy, which passes through the right nostril. The purpose of nāḍī śodhana is to balance these two flows of energy.

In the first half of the round, one inhales through the left nostril and exhales through the right. In the second half, one inhales through the right nostril and exhales through the left. This process equalises the flow of breath in both the left and right nostrils, which in turn regulates the iḍā and piṅgalā nāḍīs, the parasympathetic and sympathetic nervous system and the right and left hemispheres of the brain. Retention of the breath, as described here is an important aspect of this practice, as it activates the suṣumnā nāḍī and the central nervous system, unifying the two hemispheres of the brain. The effects of this practice on the nervous system, the pranic system and the brain, make it an important requisite for meditation and all higher sādhanas.

Here the recommended ratio, or number of mātrās, for the practice of nāḍī śodhana prāṇāyāma is given as a guideline for the advanced practitioner who has mastered the initial stages of the practice. The practitioner should first inhale slowly through the left nostril for a duration of sixteen mātrās. Next the breath should be retained inside fully for a period of sixty-four mātrās, and then exhaled through the right nostril for the duration of thirty-two mātrās.

A *mātrā* is a unit of measurement to calculate the time spent in breathing practices. It is defined in *Yoga Cūdāmani Upaniṣad* as the time a single breath takes to fill the lungs. According to *Yoga Tattva Upaniṣad* it is the time taken to snap one's fingers after circling the knee with one's hand. The *Tattva Vaiṣāradī* says one must circle the knee three times. The *Mārkandeya Purāṇa* says it is the time taken to open and close one's eyes.[26] So, inhalation for sixteen mātrās, retention for sixty-four matras, and exhalation for thirty-two mātrās, makes the ratio of 1:4:2. It must be remembered that this ratio is not the initial practice. Much training and practice are required to develop sufficient lung capacity for this ratio to be performed with comfort and ease.

The word *kumbhaka* comes from the root *kumbha*, meaning a 'vessel' or 'pot'. In order to retain the breath inside, the diaphragm expands, so that the belly forms a pot, where the air is stored for a certain time. The practice of kumbhaka, internal breath retention, activates suṣumnā, the spiritual flow of energy. In order for meditation to be successful, it is necessary to first balance the breath, which controls the mental and vital energies, and then activate suṣumnā, the spiritual force. Then the deep influx of prāṇa invigorates the body with more oxygen, eliminating toxins from the blood. It flows freely as all blockages are removed.

The symbol of anāhata cakra, the spiritual heart, is a blue lotus which represents the opening of the heart. The bīja mantra of anāhata cakra is *yaṃ*, and in its *bindu* is the presiding deity Viṣṇu.

Vāsudeva is another name for Viṣṇu. Swami Satyananda says in his book *Kundalini Tantra* that all spiritual practices will awaken devotion in the spiritual heart. [27]

The serious *sādhaka* should practise kumbhaka at the four junctions or intervals (known as *sandhya*) of dawn 4 to 6a.m., midday 11:00 am to 1:00 pm, evening 4:00 to 6:00 pm and midnight 11:00 pm to 1:00 am, as these are the times when the transition is made from one part of the day to the next. The three sandhyas (dawn, midday and dusk) are the traditional prayer times of Brahmanas. One should slowly work up to eighty breath retentions, or forty rounds.

Verses 102 to 104a: Benefits of Prāṇāyāma (1)

एकाहमात्रं कुर्वाणः सर्वपापैः प्रमुच्यते ।
संवत्सरत्रयादूर्ध्वं प्राणायामपरो नरः ॥१०२॥
योगसिद्धो भवेद्योगी वायुजिद्विजितेन्द्रियः ।
अल्पाशी स्वल्पाशी स्वल्पनिद्रश्च तेजस्वी बलवान्भवेत् ॥१०३॥
अपमृत्युमतिक्रम्य दीर्घमायुरवाप्नुयात् ।१०४।

ekāhamātraṃ kurvāṇaḥ sarvapāpaiḥ pramucyate
saṃvatsaratrayādūrdhvaṃ prāṇāyāmaparo naraḥ (102)
yogasiddho bhavedyogī vāyujidvijitendriyaḥ
alpāśī svalpāśī svalpanidraśca tejasvī balavānbhavet (103)
apamṛtyumatikramya dīrghamāyuravāpnuyāt (104a)

Vocabulary
pramucyate: one is freed; *sarva-pāpaiḥ*: from all sins; *kurvāṇaḥ*: doing; *ekāhamātram*: for one whole day; *naraḥ*: person; *prāṇāyāma-paraḥ*: absorbed in prāṇāyāma; *ūrdhvam*: upwards; *saṃvat-trayāt*: from three years; *bhavet*: becomes; *yoga-siddhaḥ*: perfected in yoga; *yogī vāyujit*: having controlled the winds; *vijita-indriyaḥ*: conquered the senses; *alpa-āśī*: eating little; *avāpnuyāt*: he achieves; *dīrgham-āyuḥ*: long life; *atikramya*: overcoming; *apamṛtyum*: sudden death.

Translation
One is freed from all sins by doing [this practice] for one whole day. The person absorbed in prāṇāyāma upwards from three years becomes perfected in yoga. The yogin, having controlled the winds [and] conquered the senses, eating little, enjoying little and sleeping little, becomes radiant and powerful. He achieves long life by overcoming sudden death.

Commentary
Here the results of the practice are given. If nāḍī śodhana is performed for three years or more* according to the method described above, the nāḍīs, or energy channels will be purified.

Purification of the nāḍīs is one of the important requisites for all the higher yogas. When the nāḍīs are purified, certain external signs manifest in the body. They are lightness of the body and increased digestive power, more energy and radiance or luminosity. The yogi who 'enjoys little' does not crave sensory pleasures. These are the signs of a yogi, one who has become adept in the practice of yoga.

* *Shandilya Upanishad* and *Yoga Darshana Upaniṣad* say three months.

Verses 104b to 110: Benefits of Prāṇāyāma (2)

प्रस्वेदजननं यस्य प्राणायामस्तु सोऽधमः ॥१०४॥
कम्पनं वपुषो यस्य प्राणायामेषु मध्यमः ।
उत्थानं वपुषो यस्य स उत्तम उदाहृतः ॥१०५॥
अधमे व्याधिपापानां नाशः स्यान्मध्यमे पुनः ।
पापतोगमहाव्याधिनाशः स्यादुत्तमे पुनः ॥१०६॥
अल्पमूत्रोऽल्पविष्ठश्च लघुदेहो मिताशनः ।
पट्विन्द्रियः पटुमतिः कालत्रयविदात्मवान् ॥१०७॥
रेचकं पूरकं मुक्त्वा कुम्भिकरणमेव यः ।
करोति त्रिषु कालेषु नैव तस्यास्ति दुर्लभम् ॥१०८॥
नाभिकन्दे च नासाग्रे पादाङ्गुष्ठे च यत्नवान् ।
धारयेन्मनसा प्राणान्सन्ध्याकालेषु वा सदा ॥१०९॥
सर्वरोगैर्विनिर्मुक्तो जीवेद्योगी गतक्लमः ।
कुक्षिरोगविनाशः स्यान्नाभिकन्देषु धारणात् ॥११०॥

prasvedajananaṃ yasya prāṇāyāmastu so'dhamaḥ (104)
kampanaṃ vapuṣo yasya prāṇāyāmeṣu madhyamaḥ
utthānaṃ vapuṣo yasya sa uttama udāhṛtaḥ (105)
adhame vyādhipāpānāṃ nāśaḥ syānmadhyame punaḥ
pāparogamahāvyādhināśaḥ syāduttame punaḥ (106)
alpamūtro'lpaviṣṭhaśca laghudeho mitāśanaḥ
paṭvindriyaḥ paṭumatiḥ kālatrayavidātmavān (107)
recakaṃ pūrakaṃ muktvā kumbhīkaraṇameva yaḥ
karoti triṣu kāleṣu naiva tasyāsti durlabham (108)
nābhikande ca nāsāgre pādāṅguṣṭhe ca yatnavān
dhārayenmanasā prāṇānsandhyākāleṣu vā sadā (109)
sarvarogairvinirmukto jīvedyogī gataklamaḥ
kukṣirogavināśaḥ syānnābhikandeṣu dhāraṇāt (110)

Vocabulary

tu udāhṛtaḥ: now it is said; *jananam*: production; *yasya*: of which; *prasveda*: perspiration; *adhamaḥ*: inferior; *prāṇāyāmeṣu*: while the prāṇāyāmas; *vapuṣaḥ yasya*:

characteristic of which; *kampanam*: shivering; *madhyamaḥ*: medium; *sa yasya*: that which has; *vapuṣaḥ*: characteristic; *utthānam*: rising; *uttama*: best; *nāśaḥ*: destruction; *vyādhi-pāpānām*: of disease and sins; *syāt*: is; *adhame*: in the inferior; *punaḥ*: again; *madhyame*: in the medium; *papa-roga-mahāvyādhi-nāśaḥ*: destruction of sins, sickness and plagues; *uttame*: in the best; *punaḥ*: as well as; *alpa-mūtraḥ*: little urine; *alpa-viṣṭhaḥ*: little excrement; *laghu-dehaḥ*: light body; *ca mita-aśanaḥ*: and a frugal diet; *ātmavān*: wise person; *paṭu-indriyaḥ*: sharp senses; *paṭu-matiḥ*: keen mind; *vid*: has knowledge of; *kāla-traya*: three stages; *yaḥ*: whoever; *karoti*: does; *karaṇam*: practice; *kumbhī*: breath retention; *muktvā*: freed from; *pūrakam recakam*: inhalation exhalation; *asti na durlabham*: can without difficulty attain; *triṣu kāleṣu*: within the three *kālas*; *yatnavān*: aspirant; *dhārayet*: should hold; *prāṇān*: prāṇas; *manasā*: by means of the mind; *nābhi-kande*: at the knot at the navel; *nāsāgre*: at the nosetip; *ca pādāṅguṣṭhe*: and at the big toes; *sadā*: always; *sandhyā-kāleṣu*: at the times of dawn, noon and dusk; *vinirmuktaḥ*: delivered; *sarva-rogaiḥ*: from all diseases; *yogī jivet*: yogin lives; *gataklamaḥ*: refreshed; *kukṣi-roga*: disease of the abdomen; *syāt vināśaḥ*: is destroyed; *dhāraṇāt*: through concentration; *nābhi-kandeṣu*: on the knot at the navel.

Translation

Now it is said [that] the prāṇāyāma, the production of which [is] perspiration [is] the [most] inferior, while the prāṇāyāmas the characteristic of which [is] shivering [is] medium [and] that which has the characteristic [of] rising [is] the best. The destruction of disease and sins is in the inferior [and] again in the medium [effect]. The destruction of sins, sickness and plagues is the best [effect], as well as little urine, little excrement, a light body and a frugal diet.

The wise person, [who has] sharp senses [and] a keen mind, has knowledge of the three stages. Whoever does the practice [of] breath retention, freed from inhalation [and] exhalation, can without difficulty attain within the three *kālas*. The aspirant should hold the prāṇas by means of the mind at the knot at the navel, the nosetip and the big toes always at the times of dawn, noon and dusk. Delivered from all diseases, the yogin lives refreshed. Disease of the abdomen is destroyed through concentration on the knot at the navel.

Commentary

Yoga Tattwa Upaniṣad says: 'At first perspiration is produced; therefore it should be cleaned. Then again, in the course of slowly holding the breath, the person experiences tremor in the body, while sitting. Then, from much more practice, frog-like sweat is produced.' [28]

The practices of prāṇāyāma rebalance the prāṇās and nervous system, preparing the body and mind for higher yogas. During the practice of kumbhaka, the yogi will experience three stages, the outer effects of which are described. At first result there is perspiration, because the practice causes the body to become heated. This perspiration is different to ordinary perspiration, and should not be washed off directly, but rather wiped off with a soft, clean cloth.

In the next stage of prāṇāyāma, trembling arises due to activation of the prāṇās, nāḍīs and nerves. In the third stage, when the practice is mastered, the prāṇas expand throughout the body and there is the experience of lightness. In this stage the body may levitate easily. When these three stages are practised repeatedly, the highest stage is attained.

Fresh milk and ghee are recommended, because they maintain the mucus lining of the digestive tract and alimentary canal and neutralise too much heat and acidity in the stomach. Kumbhaka, the retention of breath or prāṇa, is the basis of prāṇāyāma. Prāṇa is the vital energy or life force, constantly moving in all beings, and moving in and out of the body with the breath. It also flows outside, whenever the senses connect with people, places and things. Every interaction is an exchange of prāṇa. The practice of kumbhaka developed, because the yogis of old wished to conserve their prāṇa in order to awaken the consciousness. Kāla literally means time. The three kālas relate to both the three stages of kumbhaka and the three eras of past, present and future. When one has attained the three kālas, then one has transcended the limitation of time, and has entered the fourth state of consciousness, *tūriya*.

By focusing the awareness at the nose tip, while holding the breath inside, one can control the prāṇa. The nose tip forms a bridge, connecting the three major nāḍīs, iḍā, piṅgalā and suṣumnā. Therefore, by concentrating at this point, while holding the breath inside, the prāṇas can be controlled. By focusing at the navel, all diseases disappear. The navel is related with manipura cakra, where the pranic storehouse is located. When the awareness is focused at this centre, the prāṇas expand and disease disappears. When the awareness is focused at the big toes, the body becomes very light, and is capable of moving easily and quickly, because the energy is held in the proximity of the feet. By drawing the breath in through the open mouth over the tongue, holding it at maṇipura cakra, the yogin is freed from over-heating and internal toxins produced by poor diet and indigestion.

Verses 111 to 113: Benefits of Prāṇāyāma (3)

नासग्रे धारणाद्दीर्घमायुः सयाद्देहलाघवम् ।
ब्राह्मे मुहूर्ते संप्राप्ते वायुमाकृष्य जिह्वया ।।१११।।
पिबतस्त्रिषु मासेषु वाक्षिद्धिर्महती भवेत् ।
अभ्यासतश्च षण्मासान्महारोगविनाशनम् ।।११२।।
यत्र यत्र धृता वायुरङ्गे रोगादिदूषिते ।
धारणादेव मरुतस्तत्तदारोग्यमश्नुते ।।११३।।

nāsagre dhāraṇāddīrghamāyuḥ syāddehalāghavam
brāhme muhūrte saṃprāpte vāyumākṛṣya jihvayā (111)
pibatastriṣu māseṣu vāksiddhirmahatī bhavet
abhyāsataśca ṣaṇmāsānmahārogavināśanam (112)
yatra yatra dhṛtā vāyuraṅge rogādidūṣite
dhāraṇādeva marutastattadārogyamaśnute (113)

Vocabulary

dhāraṇāt: through concentration; *nāsagre*: on the nosetip; *syāt*: there is; *dīrgha-māyuḥ*: long life; *deha-lāghavam*: lightness of the body; *ākṛṣya vāyum*: having drawn in the air; *jihvayā*: through the tongue; *brāhme muhūrte saṃprāpte*: when *brahmamuhūrta* is reached; *pibataḥ*: drunk; *bhavet*: one has; *mahatī*: great; *vāk-siddhiḥ*: power of speech; *triṣu māseṣu*: within three months; *ca abhyāsataḥ*: and with regular practice; *ṣaṇ-māsān*: six months; *vināśanam*: destruction; *mahā-roga*: major disease; *yatra yatra*: wherever; *dūṣite*: there is contamination; *roga-ādi*: by disease etc; *tadā*: then; *dhṛtā dhāraṇāt*: by fixing one's concentration on; *aṅge*: limb; *vāyuḥ*: vital air; *aśnute*: has mastery over; *rogyam*: diseased area.

Translation

Through concentration on the nosetip, there is long life [and] lightness of the body. Having drawn in the air through the tongue [and] drunk[it], when *brahmamuhūrta* is reached, one has great power of speech within three months, and with regular practice for six months, [there is] destruction [of] major disease. Wherever there is contamination by disease etc, then by fixing one's concentration on that limb, the vital air has mastery over the diseased area.

Commentary

When one concentrates on the nose, the nose being the organ of smell, the *tanmātra* of mūlādhāra cakra, then mūlādhāra is awakened. One becomes free from disease and feels light, disconnected from the physical body. This is an experience of astral levitation because of the ascension of the kuṇḍalinī. [29]

Śītalī prāṇāyāma, where one draws the breath in through the tongue, which is curled around to form a tube, is a tranquilising prāṇāyāma which stimulates the parasympathetic nervous system, thus drawing the awareness inwards. It is usually practised after nāḍī śodhana when iḍā and piṅgalā, and the sympathetic and parasympathetic systems, are balanced. *Śītalī* reduces body heat. *Śīt* means cool, and *śītal* means calm and peaceful, so the practice cools body, mind and speech.

Brahma is name of the creator of the universe and *muhūrta* is a time period of 48 minutes (two *ghātikas*). So, *brahmamuhūrta* is Brahma's time, the time of sunrise when the world awakes. Brahmamuhūrta is considered to be the most auspicious time for all the spiritual practices such as yoga and meditation, and for raising the serpent power (*kuṇḍalinī śakti*).

This is the time of day when the mind is most still, free from distractions, so that one can go deep into the meditative state. The verses say that if one meditates at this time by concentrating on the nosetip, performing śītalī prāṇāyāma and then concentrating on a diseased part of the body, that part will be cured.

Verses 114 to 117: Ṣaṇmukhī Mudrā

मनसा धारणादेव पवनो धारितो भवेत् ।
मनसः स्थापने हेतुरुच्यते द्विजपुङ्गव ।।११४।।
करणानि समाहृत्य विषयेभ्यः समाहितः ।
अपानमूर्ध्वमाकृष्येदुदरोपरि धारयेत् ।।११५।।
बध्नन्कराभ्यां श्रोत्रादिकरणानि यथातथम् ।
युन्जास्य यथोक्तेन वर्त्मना स्ववशं मनः ।।११६।।
मनोवशात्प्राणवायुः स्ववशे स्थाप्यते सदा ।
नासिकापुटयोः प्राणः पर्यायेण प्रवर्तते ।।११७।।

manasā dhāraṇādeva pavano dhārito bhavet manasaḥ
sthāpane heturucyate dvijapuṅgava (114)
karaṇāni samāhṛtya viṣayebhyaḥ samāhitaḥ
apānamūrdhvamākṛṣyedudaropari dhārayet (115)
badhnankarābhyāṃ śrotrādikaraṇāni yathātatham
yunjānasya yathoktena vartmanā svavaśaṃ manaḥ (116)
manovaśātprāṇavāyuḥ svavaśe sthāpyate sadā
nāsikāpuṭayoḥ prāṇaḥ paryāyeṇa pravartate (117)

Vocabulary

eva: thus; *dhāraṇāt*: by concentration; *manasā*: through the mind; *pavanaḥ*: wind; *dhāritaḥ*: is held; *ucyate*: it is said; *hetuḥ*: means; *samāhṛtya samāhitaḥ*: for firmly establishing; *karaṇāni*: causes; *viṣayebhyaḥ*: about this matter; *sthāpane*: in the region; *manasaḥ*: of the mind; *dvijapuṅgava*: o esteemed Brāhmaṇa; *ākṛṣyet*: one should draw; *ūrdhvam apānam*: upwards the *apāna*; *dhārayet*: one should hold; *upari*: above; *udara*: abdomen; *yathātatham*: precisely; *yunjānasya*: having performed; *yathā vartmanā*: through this method; *badhnan*: binding; *śrotra-ādi*: ears and other; *karābhyām*: with the hands; *uktena*: one is said; *svavaśaṃ manaḥ*: self-controlled mind; *manaḥ-vaśāt*: by command of the mind; *prāṇa-vāyuḥ*: vital air; *sadā*: always; *sthāpyate*: is kept; *svavaśe*: under its control; *paryāyeṇa*: through [this] way; *prāṇaḥ pravartate*: *prāṇa* activates; *nāsikā-puṭayoḥ*: purification of the nostrils.

Translation

Thus by concentration through the mind the wind is held. It is said the means for firmly establishing the activities about this matter [is] in the region of the mind, o esteemed Brāhmaṇa! One should draw upwards the apāna [and] hold [it] above the abdomen. Having precisely performed through this method the binding [of] the ears and other [sense organs] with the hands, one is said [to have] a self-controlled mind. By command of the mind, the vital air is always kept under its control. Through [this] way the prāṇa activates the purification of the nostrils.

Commentary

These verses described *ṣaṇmukhī mudrā*, where the seven sensory organs (eyes, ears, nostrils and mouth) are closed with the thumbs and fingers, to induce pratyāhāra, withdrawal of the mind from the sense objects. One who has practised breath retention (kumbhaka) and nāḍī śodhana will benefit from this practice. Physical benefits are stimulation and relaxation of the facial nerves and muscles.

Technique

Sit in a meditative posture, head and spine in alignment, eyes closed, hands on knees whole body relaxed. Raise the arms in front of the face with the elbows pointing sideways. Close the ears with the thumbs, the eyes with the index fingers, the nostrils with the middle fingers, and the mouth by placing the ring and little fingers above and below the lips. Releasing the fingers from the nostrils, inhale using full yogic breathing, then close the nostrils again with the fingers. Retain the breath inside for as long as is comfortable.

You may hear sounds in the region of bindu, ājñā or anāhata cakras.
Release the fingers and exhale slowly.

This is one round. Continue.

To end the practice, slowly place the hands on the knees, keeping the eyes closed, start to externalise the mind by becoming aware of the physical body, its position and the sounds around you. Be aware of the effects of the practice on mind and body. [30]

Verses 118 to 120: Iḍā, Piṅgalā and Suṣumnā

तिस्रश्च नाडिकास्तासु स यावन्तं चरत्ययम् ।
शङ्खिनीविवरे याम्ये प्राणः प्राणभृतां सताम् ।।११८।।
तावन्तं च पुनः कालं सौम्ये चरति संततम् ।
इत्थं क्रमेण चरता वायुना वायुजिन्नरः ।।११९।।
अहश्च रात्रिं पक्षं च मासमृत्वयनादिकम् ।
अन्तर्मुखे विजानीजात्कालभेदं समाहितः ।।१२०।।

tisraśca nāḍikāstāsu sa yāvantaṃ caratyayam
śaṅkhinīvivare yāmye prāṇaḥ prāṇabhṛtāṃ satām (118)
tāvantaṃ ca punaḥ kālaṃ saumye carati saṃtatam
itthaṃ krameṇa caratā vāyunā vāyujinnaraḥ (119)
ahaśca rātriṃ pakṣaṃ ca māsamṛtvayanādikam
antarmukhe vijānīyātkālabhedaṃ samāhitaḥ (120)

Vocabulary

tisraḥ nāḍikāḥ: three nāḍīs; *tāsu*: in these; *ayam prāṇa*: this prāṇa; *prāṇa-bhṛtām*: full of energy; *satām*: continual; *carati*: moves; *yāvantam . . . tāvantam kalam*: as much . . . as it; *yāmye vivare*: through the right cave; *śaṅkhinī*: nerve; *punaḥ*: again; *saṃtatam*: continually; *carati saumye*: moves through the left; *ittham*: so; *naraḥ*: person; *vāyu-jit*: controls the vital air; *krameṇa caratā vāyunā*: by the regular flow of wind; *ahaḥ ca rātriṃ*: for a day and night; *pakṣam*: fortnight; *māsam*: month; *ca ṛtvayana-ādikam*: and other proper times; *samāhitaḥ*: steadfast; *antarmukhe*: turned inwards; *vijānīyāt*: understands; *kālabhedaṃ*: division of time.

Translation

[There are] three nāḍīs. In these this prāṇa, full of continual vital energy, moves as much through the right cave [of] the nerve as it again continually moves through the left. So the person [who] controls the vital air by the regular flow of wind for a day and night, fortnight, month and other proper times, [whose mind is] steadfast, turned inwards, understands the division of time.

Commentary

The three nāḍīs are iḍā, piṅgalā and suṣumnā. Through the practices of prāṇāyāma the prāṇa, which is continually flowing through the left and right main nāḍīs, iḍā and piṅgalā, can be controlled so that they are balanced. Neither will have a stronger or weaker flow than the other.

Through them the lunar and solar currents run. Just as the external moon dominates our internal perception of night, so iḍā, *candra nāḍī*, the internal moon, is dominant at night when the parasympathetic nervous system and the subconscious mind are active. Just as we are under the influence of the external sun during the day, so piṅgalā, *sūrya nāḍī*, is dominant in the day when the sympathetic nervous system is more active, the mind is externalised and the body energised.

So the biological system is subject to the twenty-four hour cycles of sun and moon. Suṣumnā nāḍī is the channel for awakening spiritual consciousness. Within suṣumnā are these three nāḍīs: *vajriṇī, citriṇī* and *brahma. Brahma nāḍī*, the most interior and subtle one, is the one in which the *kuṇḍalinī śakti* ascends. It is possible, through consistent daily practices of prāṇāyāma, such as nāḍī śodhana and ṣaṇmukhī mudrā, to control the prāṇa so that it flows equally in iḍā and piṅgalā, activating suṣumnā nāḍī and ājñā cakra, going beyond the duality of both time and space. This is called *akhanda kāla*, endless time. Through the formation of the five tattwas (ether, air, fire, water earth) comes transitory time. When the kuṇḍalinī śakti in mūlādhāra is released through suṣumnā, śakti is moving back to its original infinite state. Arthur Avalon in his book The Serpent Power says 'suṣumnā devours kāla. For on that path entry is made into timelessness'. [31]

Verses 121 to 129a: Signs of Approaching Death

अङ्गुष्ठादिस्वावयवस्फुरणादर्शनैरपि ।
अरिष्टैर्जीवितस्यापि जानीयात्क्षयमात्मनः ॥१२१॥
ज्ञात्वा यतेत कैवल्यप्राप्तये योगवित्तमः ।
पादाङ्गुष्ठे कराङ्गुष्ठे स्फुरणं यस्य स्रुति ॥१२२॥
तस्य संवत्सरादूर्ध्वं जीवितस्य क्षयो भवेत् ।
मणिबन्धे तथा गुल्फे स्फुरणं यस्य नश्यति ॥१२३॥
षण्मासावधिरेतस्य जीवितस्य स्थितिर्भवेत् ।
कूर्परे स्फुरणं यस्य तस्य त्रैमासिकी स्थितिः ॥१२४॥
कुक्षिमुहनपार्श्वे च स्फुरणानुपलम्भने ।
मासावधिर्जीवितस्य तदर्धस्य तु दर्शने ॥१२५॥
आश्रिते हठरद्वारे दिनानि दश जीवितम् ।
ज्योतिः खद्योतवद्यस्य तदर्धं तस्य जीवितम् ॥१२६॥
जिह्वाग्रादर्शने त्रीणि दिनानि स्थितिरात्मनः ।
ज्वालाय दर्शने मृतुर्द्विदिने भवति ध्रुवम् ॥१२७॥
एवमादीन्यरिष्टानि दृष्टायुः क्षयकारणम् ।
निःश्रेयसाय युञ्जीत जपध्यानपरायणः ॥१२८॥
मनसा परमात्मानं ध्यात्वा तद्रूपतामियात् ।१२९।

aṅguṣṭhādisvāvayasphuraṇādarśanairapi
ariṣṭairjīvitasyāpi jānīyātkṣayamātmanaḥ (121)
jñātvā yateta kaivalyaprāptaye yogavittamaṃ
pādāṅguṣṭhe karāṅguṣṭhe sphuraṇaṃ yasya sruti (122)
tasya saṃvatsarādūrdhvaṃ jīvitasya kṣayo bhavet
maṇibandhe tathā gulphe sphuraṇaṃ yasya naśyati (123)
ṣaṇmāsāvadhiretasya jīvitasya sthirbhavet
kūrpare sphuraṇaṃ yasya tasya traimāsikī sthitiḥ (124)
kukṣimehanapārśve ca sphuraṇānupalambhane
māsāvadhirjīvitasya tadardhasya tu darśane (125)
āśrite jaṭharadvāre dināni daśa jīvitam

jyotiḥ khadyotavadyasya tadardhaṃ tasya jīvitam (126)
jihvāgrādarśane trīṇi dināni sthitirātmanaḥ
jvālāya darśane mṛtyurdvidine bhavati dhruvam (127)
evamādīnyariṣṭāni dṛṣṭāyuḥ kṣayakāraṇam
niḥśreyasāya yuñjīta japadhyānaparāyaṇaḥ (128)
manasā paramātmānaṃ dhyātvā tadrūpatāmiyāt (129a)

Vocabulary

adarśanaiḥ: disappearance; *sphuraṇa*: vibration; *svāvaya*: one's vital airs; *aṅguṣṭha-ādi*: in the thumbs and other; *api . . api ariṣṭaiḥ*: as well as forebodings; *jīvitasya*: about his life; *jānīyāt*: he knows; *kṣayam-ātmanaḥ*: end of his self; *jñātvā yat*: knowing this; *yoga-vittamaṃ*: highest knowledge of yoga; *kaivalya-prāptaye*: should reach *kaivalya*; *kṣayaḥ*: end; *tasya jīvitasya*: of his life; *bhavet*: will be; *saṃvatsarāt-ūrdhvam*: in a year or more; *yasya sphuraṇam*: when the vibration; *pādāṅguṣṭhe karāṅguṣṭhe*: in the feet [and] hands; *sruti*: fades away; *tathā*: similarly; *yasya sphuraṇam*: when the vibration; *maṇibandhe gulphe*: in the wrist [and] ankle; *naśyati*: disappears; *sthiḥ-bhavet*: there will remain; *ṣaṇmāsa-avadhiḥ*: limit of six months; *etasya jīvitasya*: of his life; *tasya sthitiḥ*: his stay; *traimāsikī*: lasts three months; *yasya sphuraṇam*: when the vibration; *kūrpare*: in the elbow; *anupalambhane*: if no evidence; *sphuraṇa*: vibration; *darśane*: is seen; *pārśve*: near; *kukṣi-mehana*: abdomen [and] genitals; *māsā-vadhiḥ*: within a month; *tu*: then; *ardhasya jīvitasya*: half his life; *āśrite*: if there is; *jaṭhara-dvāre*: at the entrance to the stomach; *daśa dināni*: ten days; *jīvitam*: life; *tat-ardhaṃ jīvitam*: this half-life; *jyotiḥ*: light; *dyotavat*: illuminating; *kha*: sky; *jihvāgra*: tip of the tongue; *adarśane*: when . . is not seen; *sthitiḥ-ātmanaḥ*: remainder [of] the self; *trīṇi dināni*: three days; *jvālāya darśane*: when a flame is seen; *mṛtyuḥ*: death; *bhavati dhruvam*: is definite; *dvidine*: in two days; *dṛṣṭāyuḥ*: having seen; *evamādīni-ariṣṭāni*: such signs; *kṣayakāraṇam*: destruction; *yuñjīta*: he should prepare

himself; *niḥśreyasāya*: for the ultimate bliss; *parāyaṇaḥ*: by intent practice; *japa-dhyāna*: *japa* [and] meditation; *dhyātvā*: having meditated on; *paramātmānam*: Supreme Self; *manasā*:

through the mind; *iyāt*: he attains; *tad-rūpatām*: state of that form.

Translation

By the disappearance of the vibration of the yogin's vital airs in the thumbs and other [limbs] as well as forebodings about his life, he knows the end of his self. Knowing this, [whoever has] the highest knowledge of yoga should reach kaivalya. The end of his life will be in a year or more when the vibration in the feet and hands fades away. Similarly when the vibration in the wrist and ankle disappears, there will remain a limit of six months of his life. His stay [in the world] lasts three months when the vibration in the elbow [disappears]. If no evidence [of any] vibration is seen near the abdomen and genitals, then within a month, half his life [is gone]. If there is [no vibration] at the entrance to the stomach, [there remains] ten days [of] life, then this half-life is a light illuminating the sky. When the tip of the tongue is not seen, the remainder of the self [is] three days. When a flame is seen, death is definite in two days. Having seen such signs [of] destruction, he should prepare himself for the ultimate bliss by intent practice [of] *japa* and meditation. Having meditated on the Supreme Self through the mind, he attains the state of that form.

Commentary

These verses give the signs of impending death. In the time before a person dies, the circulation reduces so that blood is directed to the internal organs. Therefore very little prāṇa is still flowing to fingers, hands, toes, feet and other limbs. This may be experienced as cold or numbness. The signs are listed, not to strike fear in the aspiring yogin, but to encourage him or her to devote the remaining time to *japa*, repetition of mantra, and meditation, thus attaining *kaivalya*, final liberation.

Each sign predicts how much earthly time remains. A year remains when there is less prāṇa flowing to the feet and hands. A maximum of six months remains when there is no prāṇa in the wrists and ankles. Only three months remain when there is no prāṇa in the elbows. A month remains when there is no prāṇa near the abdomen and genitals. When there is no digestion, ten days remain. When the tip of the tongue is not visible, three days remain. When the yogin sees a flame, he will leave his earthly body within two days. Having consistently and devotedly meditated, he will merge with *paramātman*, the Supreme Self.

Verses 129b to 134: Pratyāhāra Leads to Dhāraṇā

यद्यष्टादशभेदेषु मर्मस्थानेषु धारणम् ॥१२९॥
स्थानात्स्थानं समाकृष्य प्रत्याहारः स उच्यते ।
पादाङ्गुष्ठं तथा गुल्फं जङ्घामध्यं तथैव च ॥१३०॥
मध्यमूर्वोश्च मूलं च पायुर्हृदयमेव च ।
मेहनं देहमध्यं च नाभिं च गलकूर्परम् ॥१३१॥
तालुमूलं च मूलं च घ्राणस्याक्ष्णोश्च मण्डलम् ।
भ्रुवोर्मध्यं ललाटं च मूलमूर्ध्वं च जानुनी ॥१३२॥
मूलं च करयोर्मूलं महान्त्येतानि वै द्विज ।
पञ्चभूतमये देहे भूतेष्वेतेषु पञ्चसु ॥१३३॥
मनसा धारणं यत्तद्युक्तस्य च यमादिभिः ।
धारणा सा च संसारसागरोत्तारणम् ॥१३४॥

yadyaṣṭādaśabhedeṣu marmasthāneṣu dhāraṇam (129b)
sthānātsthānaṃ samākṛṣya pratyāhāraḥ sa ucyate
pādāṅguṣṭhaṃ tathā gulphaṃ jaṅghāmadhyaṃ tathaiva ca (130)
madhyamūrvośca mūlaṃ ca pāyurhṛdayameva ca
mehanaṃ dehamadhyaṃ ca nābhiṃ ca galakūrparam (131)
tālumūlaṃ ca mūlaṃ ca ghrāṇasyākṣṇośca maṇḍalam
bhruvormadhyaṃ lalāṭaṃ ca mūlamūrdhvaṃ ca jānunī (132)
mūlaṃ ca karayormūlaṃ mahāntyetāni vai dvija
pañcabhūtamaye dehe bhūteṣveteṣu pañcasu (133)
manasā dhāraṇaṃ yattadyuktasya ca yamādibhiḥ
dhāraṇā sā ca saṃsārasāgarottārakāraṇam (134)

Vocabulary

yadi: if; *dhāraṇam*: holding; *aṣṭādaśa-bhedeṣu*: on the eighteen different; *marma-sthāneṣu*: seats of *marman*; *samākṛṣya*: withdrawing; *sthānāt-sthānam*: from seat to seat; *ucyate pratyāhāraḥ*: is called *pratyāhāra*; *tathā*: thus; *pādāṅguṣṭham*: big toes; *gulpham*: ankles; *ca tathaiva*: and in the same manner; *jaṅghā-madhyam*: middle of the shanks;

madhyam-ūrvoḥ: middle of the thighs; *ca mūlam*: and [their] base; *pāyuḥ-hṛdayam*: anus and heart; *mehanam*: genitals; *deha-madhyam*: middle of the body; *nābhim*: navel; *gala*: throat; *kūrparam*: elbows; *tālu-mūlam*: root of the palate; *ca mūlam ghrāṇasya*: and the root of the nose; *maṇḍalam*: region; *akṣṇoḥ*: of the eyes; *bhruvoḥ-madhyam*: eyebrow centre; *mūlam-ūrdhvam*: base and top; *lalāṭam*: forehead; *mūlam jānunī*: root [of] the knees; *ca karayoḥ-mūlam*: and the root of the hands; *etāni*: these; *dvija*: o Twice-Born; *eteṣu pañcasu bhūteṣu*: in these five elements; *dehe*: in the body; *mahānti pañca-bhūta*: five great elements; *yat . . . tat*: once . . then; *dhāraṇam*: concentration; *manasā*: through the mind; *yuktasya*: established; *ca yama-ādibhiḥ*: by the *yamas* and other; *kāraṇam*: cause; *uttāra*: crossing; *sāgara*: ocean; *saṃsāra*: worldly existence.

Translation

If [there is] the holding [of the vital air] on the eighteen different seats of *marman*, withdrawing from seat to seat is called *pratyāhāra*. Thus the big toes, the ankles and in the same manner the middle of the shanks, the middle of the thighs and their base, the anus and the heart, the genitals, the middle of the body, the navel, the throat, elbows, the root of the palate and the root of the nose, the region of the eyes, the eyebrow centre, the base and top [of] the forehead, the root [of] the knees and of the hands, these, o Twice-Born, [are the seats] in the five great elements. Once concentration through the mind on the five elements in the body [is] established by the *yamas* and other [limbs of yoga], then [there is] *dhāraṇā*, the cause of the crossing [of] the ocean [of] worldly existence.

Commentary

The 'eighteen seats of *marman*' are the most vulnerable points of the body, according to *āyurveda* ('knowledge of life'), the original Indian system of health and healing. It is said that knowledge of acupuncture points comes from āyurveda. Marma points are specific anatomical locations through which the energy of the five elements flow. They can be stimulated by the technique of marma massage or by concentrating the prāṇa on these locations. Focussing the attention and breath on each marman releases it from tensions so that the life-force, prāṇa, can flow freely through the subtle channels (nāḍīs). [32]

Verses 135 to 145a: Meditation on the Five Elements

आजानुपादपर्यन्तं पृथिवीस्थानमिष्यते ।
पित्तला चतुरस्रा च वसुधा वज्रलाञ्छता ॥१३५॥
स्मर्तव्या पञ्चघटिकास्त्रारोप्य प्रभञ्जनम् ।
आजानुकटिपर्यन्तमपां स्थानं प्रकीर्तितम् ॥१३६॥
अर्धचन्द्रसमाकारं श्वेतमर्जुनलाच्छितम् ।
स्मर्तव्यमम्भःश्वसनमारोप्य दश नाडिकाः ॥१३७।
आदेहमध्यकट्यन्तमग्निस्थानमुदाहृतम् ।
तत्र सिन्धूरवर्णोऽग्निर्ज्वलनं दश पञ्च च ॥१३८॥
स्मर्तव्या नाडिकाः प्राणं कृत्वा कुम्भे तथेरिताम् ।
नाभेरुपारि नासान्तं वायुस्थानं तु तत्र वै ॥१३९॥
वेदिकाकारवद्धूम्रो बलवान्भूतमारुतः ।
स्मर्तव्यः कुम्भकेनैव प्राणमारोपय मारुतम् ॥१४०॥
घटिकाविंशतिस्तस्माद् घ्राणाद्ब्रह्मबिलावधि ।
व्योमस्थानं नभस्तत्र बिन्नाञ्जनसमप्रभम् ॥१४१॥
व्योम्नि नारुतमारोप्य कुम्भकेनैव यत्नवान् ।१४२।
पृथिव्यंशे तु देहस्य चतुर्बाहुं किरीटिनम् ॥१४२॥
अनिरुद्धं हरिं योगी यतेत भवमुक्तये ।
अबंशे पूरयेद्योगी नारायणमुदग्रधीः ॥१४३॥
प्रद्युम्नमग्नौ वाय्वंशे संकर्षणमतः परम् ।
व्योमांशे परमात्मानं वासुदेवं सदा स्मरेत् ॥१४४॥
आचिरादेव तत्प्राप्तिर्युञ्जानस्य न संशयः ।१४५।

ājānupādaparyantaṃ pṛthivīsthānamiṣyate pittalā caturasrā ca vasudhā vajralāñchatā (135)
smartavyā pañcaghaṭikāstatrāropya prabhañjanam ājānukaṭiparyantamapāṃ sthānaṃ prakīrtitam (136)
ardhacandrasamākāraṃ śvetamarjunalācchitam

smartavyamambhaḥśvasanamāropya daśa nāḍikāḥ (137)
ādehamadhyakaṭyantamagnisthānamudāhṛtam
tatra sindhūravarṇe'gnirjvalanaṃ daśa pañca ca (138)
smartavyā nāḍikāḥ prāṇaṃ kṛtvā kumbha tatheritam
nābherupari nāsāntaṃ vāyusthānaṃ tu tatra vai (139)
vedikākāravaddhūmro balavānbhūtamārutaḥ
smartavyaḥ kumbhakenaiva prāṇamāropya mārutam (140)
ghaṭikāviṃśatistasmād ghrāṇādbrahmabilāvadhi
vyomasthānaṃ nabhastatra binnāñjanasamaprabham (141)
vyomni mārutamāropya kumbhakenaiva yatnavān
pṛthvyaṃśe tu dehasya caturbāhuṃ kirīṭinam (142)
aniruddhaṃ hariṃ yogī yateta bhavamuktaye
abaṃśe pūrayedyogī nārāyaṇamudagradhīḥ (143)
pradyumnamagnau vāyvaṃśe saṃkarṣaṇamataḥ param
vyomāṃśe paramātmānaṃ vāsudevaṃ sadā smaret (144)
ācirādeva tatprāptiryuñjānasya na saṃśayaḥ (145a)

Vocabulary

pṛthivī-sthānam: seat of earth; *iṣyate*: goes; *pāda*: feet; *paryantam*: right up to; *ājānu*: knees; *vasudhā*: earth; *pittalā*: yellow; *ca caturasrā*: and square; *vajra-lāñchatā*: sign of the diamond; *smartavyā*: to be meditated on; *pañca-ghaṭikās*: five *ghaṭikās* (two hours); *āropya*: having filled; *prabhañjanam*: vital air; *sthānam apāṃ*: seat of water; *prakīrtitam*: is said; *ājānu*: knees; *kaṭi-paryantam*: right up to the waist; *ambhaḥ*: water; *samākāram*: like; *ardhacandra*: crescent moon; *lācchitam*: mark; *śvetam-arjuna*: silver and white; *smartavyam*: should be contemplated; *daśa nāḍikās*: ten *nāḍikās*; *śvasanam*: wind; *āropya*: having been inhaled; *ādeha-madhya*: from the middle of the body; *kaṭi-antam*: down to the hip; *audāhṛtam*: is called; *agni-sthānam*: place of fire; *tatra*: there; *kṛtvā kumbha*: having been retained; *sindhūra-varṇe*: vermilion-coloured; *agniḥ-jvalanam*: blazing fire; *smartavyā*: should be meditated on; *daśa pañca nāḍikās*: fifteen *nāḍikās*; *tatheritam*: so it is said.

vāyu-sthānam: seat of air; *tatra*: there; *nābheḥ-upari*: from above the navel; *nāsā-antam*: up to the nose; *balavān-bhūta-mārutaḥ*: strong element of air; *dhūmraḥ*: smoke-coloured; *vedikā-ākāravad*: with the shape of an altar; *tasmāt*: thus; *smartavyaḥ*: should be meditated on; *ghaṭikā-viṃśatiḥ*: for twenty *ghaṭikās*; *prāṇam-āropya*: prāṇa having been inhaled; *kumbhakena*: with retention at; *mārutam*: vital air; *ghrāṇāt*: from the nose; *brahmabila-avadhi*: up to the crown of the head; *vyoma-sthānam*: seat of ether; *nabhaḥ-tatra*: ether there; *samaprabham*: as bright as; *binnāñjana*: pounded antimony; *mārutam-āropya*: having inhaled the vital air; *kumbhakena vyomni*: with retention in ether; *yatnavān*: with great effort.

aṃśe: in the part; *dehasya*: of the body; *pṛthvi*: earth element; *yogī yateta*: yogin should endeavour; *bhava-muktaye*: to free himself from mundane existence; *aniruddham harim*: Aniruddha and Viṣṇu; *caturbāhum*: four-armed; *kirīṭinam*: adorned with a crown; *yogī pūrayet*: yogin should inhale deeply; *udagra-dhīḥ*: mind exalted; *sadā smaret nārāyaṇam*: should always meditate on Nārāyaṇa; *abiṃśe*: in the region of the water element; *pradyumnam-agnau*: Pradyumna in the fire element; *saṃkarṣaṇa vāyu-aṃśe*: in the region of the air element; *ataḥ param*: next; *paramātmānam vāsudevam*: Supreme Self Vāsudeva; *vyoma-aṃśe*: in the region of the ether element; *na saṃśayaḥ*: no doubt; *tat*: that; *yuñjānasya*: yogin; *prāptiḥ*: will attain; *ācirāt*: in a short time.

Translation

The seat of earth goes [from] the feet right up to the knees. Earth, yellow and square, the sign of the diamond, [is] to be meditated on for five *ghaṭikās* (two hours), having been filled with vital air. The seat of water is said [to be from] the knees right up to the waist. Water like the [shape of] the crescent moon, [whose] mark [is] silver and white, should be contemplated on for ten *nāḍikās*, the wind having been inhaled [there]. From the middle of the body down to the hip is called the place of fire. There, the prāṇa having been retained, the

vermilion-coloured blazing fire should be meditated on for fifteen nāḍikās, so it is said.
The seat of air [is] there from above the navel up to the nose. The strong element of air, smoke-coloured, with the shape of an altar, should thus be meditated on for twenty ghaṭikās (eight hours), the prāṇa having been inhaled with retention at [the seat of] vital air. From the nose up to the crown of the head [is] the seat of ether. The ether there [is] as bright as pounded antimony. Having inhaled the vital air with retention in ether, [one should hold it there] with great effort.

In the part of the body [which is] the earth element, the yogin should endeavour to free himself from mundane existence [by meditating on] Aniruddha [and] four-armed Viṣṇu adorned with a crown. The yogin should inhale deeply, [and] always meditate, his mind exalted, on Nārāyaṇa in the region of the water element, Pradyumna in the fire element, Samkarsana in the region of the air element, [and] next the Supreme Self, Vāsudeva, in the region of the ether element. [There is] no doubt that the yogin will attain in a short time.

Commentary
These verses describe the symbols of the five elements, their locations in the body and ways of meditating on them. The location of *pṛthvi*, the earth element, in the physical body is in-between the toes and the knees. The symbol that invokes this energy is a large yellow square or diamond. Yellow is the colour of earth and the square represents its solid and substantial nature. A diamond is the hardest known natural material, formed deep in the earth. In order to meditate on the earth element, the yogin should direct the awareness into the region between the knees and the toes and here visualise a large brilliant square yellow diamond.

Mentally trace its four sides, inhaling up one side, exhaling down the next, and so on. By meditating regularly in this

way for a duration of two hours, the earth element will be purified and strengthened.
The location of *āpas*, the water element, in the body is in-between the knees and the navel. The symbol of water is a white crescent moon. The moon is the symbol of water, because it relates with the tides and thus controls the seas. The colour of āpas is white, which represents purity, as water washes all things clean.

In order to meditate on the water element, the yogin should first direct the awareness into the region between the navel and the knees. Here the white crescent moon should be visualised. See the white colour. Feel the fluid quality and the coolness. Then rotate the breath together with the awareness, inhaling along the upper curve of the crescent moon from left to right, and then exhaling along the lower curve from right to left. By meditating regularly in this way for a duration of four hours, the water element will be purified and strengthened.

The location of *agni*, the fire element, is from the navel to the heart. The symbol of agni is a fiery red, inverted triangle, with the lower angle at the navel, and the upper two angles parallel with the heart. In order to meditate on the fire element, the practitioner should direct the awareness to this region between the navel and the heart. Visualise the radiant red, inverted triangle, filling this entire region with heat and light. Rotate the awareness along the three sides of the triangle, starting at the navel. Ascend along the right side, then cross over the top parallel to the heart, and descend along the left side. When this practice becomes familiar, add the rotation of the breath. Inhale up the right side, then hold the breath inside while moving across the top of the triangle, and exhale down the left side. By meditating in this way regularly for a period of six hours, the fire element is strengthened and purified.

The symbol of *vāyu,* the air element, is a blue hexagon. The verse says it is located from above the navel up to the nose. *Tattwa Shuddhi* and *Yoga Tattwa Upanishad* both say its physical position is between the heart and the eyebrow centre. [33] Visualise the form of a large blue hexagon, filling this entire space. See one point of the hexagon at the heart, a second point at the eyebrow centre, and two points to either side. Rotate the awareness around the six sides of the hexagon in a clockwise direction, seeing each side clearly. When the placement of the six sides of the hexagon is seen clearly, begin to rotate the breath along with the awareness, inhaling upward along the three sides to the right, and then exhaling downward along the three sides to the left. By meditating regularly in this way for a duration of eight hours, the air element will be purified and strengthened.

Ākāśa, ether, or space, is the subtlest element, and is also the vehicle of consciousness. The location of ākāśa in the physical body is between the eyebrow centre and the crown of the head. The symbol for space is a circle, which has no beginning and no end. The colour of the circle is said here to be smoky-grey. Other texts describe it as black, white or multi-coloured. The colour of the circle represents the void, which has no colour, and yet contains the potential of all colours. The circle of the void fills the space above the eyebrows, The yogin should direct his awareness into the space above the eyebrows, and visualise the circle of the void. Seeing the circumference of the circle clearly, he should rotate the awareness around it in a clockwise direction. When this rotation becomes effortless, he should add the awareness of the breath, so that each inhalation is one complete rotation of the circle and each exhalation is the next rotation.

The yogin should also meditate on the deities of the elements to attain liberation. It is said in the *Śānti Parva*[34] that Aniruddha, Pradyumna, Saṃkarṣana and Vāsudeva are the *caturvyūhas* (four forms) of Lord Viṣṇu, who pervades all, and that Nārāyaṇa is the Supreme Soul without attributes.

Nārāyaṇa is another epithet of Viṣṇu, associated with water. To meditate on Viṣṇu in all of his forms, visualise him as tall and slender with glistening black hair, a creamy or pale blue complexion and perfect symmetrical features.

Verses 145b to 149a: Meditating on Vāsudeva

बद्धवा योगासनं पूर्वं हृद्देशे हृदयाञ्जलिः ।।१४५।।
नासाग्रन्यस्तनयनो जिह्वां कृत्वा च तालुनि ।
दन्तैर्दन्तानसंस्पृश्य उर्ध्वकायः समाहितः ।।१४६।।
संयमेच्चेन्द्रियग्राममात्मबुद्ध्या विशुद्धया ।
चिन्तनं वासुदेवस्य परस्य परमात्मनः ।।१४७।।
स्वरूपव्याप्तरूपस्य ध्यानं कैवल्यसिद्धिदम् ।
याममात्रं वासुदेवं दिन्तयेत्कुम्भकेन यः ।।१४८।।
सप्तजन्मार्जितं पापं तस्य नश्यति योगिनः ।१४९।

baddhavā yogāsanaṃ pūrvaṃ hṛddeśe hṛdayāñjaliḥ (145b)
nāsāgranyastanayano jihvāṃ kṛtvā ca tāluni
dantairdantānasaṃspṛśya ūrdhvakāyaḥ samāhitaḥ (146)
saṃyameccendriyagrāmamātmabuddhyā viśuddhayā
cintanaṃ vāsudevasya parasya paramātmanaḥ (147)
svarūpavyāptarūpasya dhyānaṃ kaivalyasiddhidam
yāmamātraṃ vāsudevaṃ cintayetkumbhakena yaḥ (148)
saptajanmārjitaṃ pāpaṃ tasya naśyati yoginaḥ (149a)

Vocabulary

baddhavā yogāsanam: firmly settled in *yogāsana*; *pūrvam*: as before; *hṛdayāñjaliḥ*: *hṛdayāñjali mudrā*; *hṛd-deśe*: in the region of the heart; *nayanaḥ*: eyes; *nyasta*: fixed on; *nāsāgra*: nosetip; *ca kṛtvā*: and having placed; *jihvām*: tongue; *tāluni*: on the palate; *asaṃspṛśya*: not touching; *dantān*: teeth; *dantaiḥ*: with teeth; *ūrdhva-kāyaḥ*: body upright; *samāhitaḥ*: steadfast; *saṃyamet*: he should restrain; *indriyagrāmam*: all sense organs; *viśuddhayā*: purifying; *ātma-buddhyā*: attaining knowledge of the Self; *cintanam*: reflecting; *parasya vāsudevasya*: on the Supreme Vāsudeva; *paramātmanaḥ*: Transcendent Self; *dhyānam*: meditating on; *rūpasya*: whose form; *vyāpta*: has pervaded; *svarūpa*: one's own form; *kaivalya-siddhidam*: power of final liberation; *yoginaḥ yaḥ*: yogin who; *cintayet vāsudevam*: reflects on Vāsudeva; *yāma-*

mātram: for one *yāma*, three hours; *kumbhakena*: with breath restraint; *naśyati*: will erase; *pāpam*: sins; *sapta-janma-arjitam*: seven previous births.

Translation

Firmly settled in *yogāsana* as before, the *hṛdayāñjali mudrā* in the region of the heart, eyes fixed on the nosetip, and having placed the tongue on the palate, not touching teeth with teeth, body upright, steadfast, he should restrain all sense organs, purifying [the mind and] attaining knowledge of the Self. Reflecting on the Supreme Vāsudeva, the Transcendent Self, meditating on [Him] whose form has pervaded one's own form [he has] the power of final liberation. That yogin, who reflects on Vāsudeva for one *yāma* with breath restraint, will erase the sins [of] seven previous births.

Commentary

These verses describe the process of meditating on Vāsudeva, the Transcendent Self. The yogin should assume one of the meditation postures such as svastikāsana, siddhāsana or padmāsana, so that the head, neck and spine are erect and in alignment, the knees are resting on the floor and mūlādhāra cakra is stimulated. In this way the body provides its own seat so that one can sit comfortably without moving for some time.

In *hṛdayāñjali mudrā* the palms of the hands are brought together with the extended fingers pointing upward, and held at the heart cakra, thumbs resting lightly against the sternum, to welcome the deity. 'According to the yogic tradition, the individual soul resides in *hṛdayākaśa* (space of the heart) in the form of a flame or point of light.'[35] This flame is quite still, unaffected by emotions and desires, and represents the spirit, the true Self, which is beyond mind and body.

Khecarī mudrā should be assumed where the tongue is folded back so that its under-surface rests against the upper palate and the upper and lower rows of teeth are slightly apart. This mudrā reduces hunger and thirst, produces feelings of inner calm and stillness and conserves energy.[36]

Then the yogin should practise pratyāhāra, withdrawal of the senses from external sense objects, so that he can concentrate first on the form of Vāsudeva, tall and strong with lustrous black hair and beard, then going beyond the form and recognising the Transcendental Self, beyond form, known as Vāsudeva, permeating his own body. Whoever can practise kumbhaka, breath retention, for three hours while engrossed in meditation on Vāsudeva, will eliminate the karma of wrong-doings of his seven previous births.

Verse 149b to 152a: States of Awareness

नाभिकन्दात्समारभ्य यावद्धृदयगोचरम् ।।१४९।।
जाग्रद्वृत्तिं विजानीयात्कण्ठस्थं स्वप्नवर्तनम् ।
सुषुप्तं तालुमध्यस्थं तुर्यं भ्रूमध्यसंस्थितम् ।।१५०।।
तुर्यातीतं परं ब्रह्म ब्रह्मरन्ध्रे तु लक्षयेत् ।
जाग्रद्वृत्तिं समारभ्य यावद्ब्रह्मबिलान्तरम् ।।१५१।।
तत्रात्मायं तुरीयस्य तुर्यन्ते विष्णुरुच्यते ।१५२।

nābhikandātsamārabhya yāvaddhṛdayagocaram (149b)
jāgradvṛttiṃ vijānīyātkaṇṭhasthaṃ svapnavartanam
suṣuptaṃ tālumadhyasthaṃ turyaṃ bhrūmadhyasaṃsthitam (150)
turyātītaṃ paraṃ brahma brahmarandre tu lakṣayet
jāgradvṛttiṃ samārabhya yāvadbrahmabilāntaram (151)
tatrātmāyaṃ turīyasya turyante viṣṇurucyate (152a)

Vocabulary

samārabhya: beginning; *nābhi-kandāt*: from the knot of the navel; *yāvad*: up to; *hṛdaya-gocaram*: region of the heart; *jāgrat-vṛttim*: waking state; *vijānīyāt*: from there; *kaṇṭha-stham*: area of the throat; *svapna-vartanam*: state of dreaming; *suṣuptam*: deep sleep; *tālu-madhya-stham*: in the middle of the palate; *bhrūmadhya-saṃsthitam*: is fixed at the eyebrow centre; *lakṣayet*: one perceives; *turya-atītam*: what is beyond turya; *paraṃ brahma*: Supreme Brahma; *brahmarandre*: *brahmarandra*; *samārabhya*: beginning from; *jāgrat-vṛttim*: waking state; *yāvad*: up to; *brahmabila-antaram*: crevice of Brahma; *tatra*: there; *ātma-ayaṃ turīyasya*: seer of turīya; *turyante*: end of turya; *viṣṇuḥ-ucyate*: is said [to be] Viṣṇu.

Translation

[The place] beginning from the knot of the navel up to the region of the heart [is] the waking state. From there the state of dreaming is in the area of the throat. Deep sleep [is] in the middle of the palate [and] turīya, the fourth state, is fixed at the eyebrow centre. One perceives what is beyond *turīya*, the Supreme Brahman, in the *brahmarandra*, beginning from the waking state up to the crevice of Brahman. There [is] the seer of turīya, the end of which is said [to be] Viṣṇu.

Commentary

These verses describe how the four states of consciousness relate to the cakras.

The two lower cakras, mūlādhāra and svādiṣṭhāna, are of the quality of tamas, meaning stability and inertia. The waking state relates to maṇipura cakra, which has the quality of rajas, meaning activity and dynamism. Pranic energy is distributed by maṇipura throughout the whole body. Many Buddhist and tantric texts say that the actual awakening of kuṇḍalinī takes place from maṇipura, because, as awakening here is continuous, there is no danger of falling back to the lower cakras. When kuṇḍalinī reaches anāhata cakra, it stays there for some time, as it is in *hṛdayākaśa*, the heart space, which is connected with the part of the brain responsible for creativity including the fine arts.

So the state of dreaming starts at anāhata and continues up to viśuddhi cakra at the throat, the basis for *vijñānamaya koṣa*, the body of intuition and psychic perception.

Deep sleep, where there is no external or internal awareness, is in the middle of the palate towards the uvula at *tālu-mūla*, also known as *lalanā cakra*, a minor cakra between viśuddhi and ājñā. When the nectar drips down from bindu it is stored in lalanā, where it is neither nectar nor poison.

Turīya, the fourth dimension of consciousness which pervades the other three states, is located at ājñā cakra at the eyebrow centre, where the three main nāḍīs, iḍā, piṅgalā and suṣumnā, merge into one stream of consciousness, and flow up to sahasrāra, the crown cakra. Here at ājñā cakra there is a high level of awareness and intuition, detachment from sensorial experiences and understanding of cause and effect.

Once the yogin is fully aware of the four states of consciousness, he transcends the fourth state, ascending to Brahman at the crown of the head, and finally attains *turīya-atīta*, 'that which transcends the fourth' or 'seer of turīya', the condition of living liberation, and realisation of Viṣṇu. [37]

Verses 152b to 156a: Meditation on Viṣṇu and the Universe

ध्यानेनैव समायुक्तो व्योम्नि चात्यन्तनिर्मले ।।१५२।।
सूर्यकोटिद्युतिधरं नित्योदितमदोक्षजम् ।
हृदयाम्बुरुहासीनं ध्यायेद्वा विश्वरूपिणम् ।।१५३।।
आनेकाकार खचितमनेकवदनान्वितम् ।
अनेकभुजसंयुक्तमनेकायुधमण्डितम् ।।१५४।।
नानावर्णधरं देवं शान्तमुग्रमुदायुधम् ।
अनेकनयनाकीर्णं सूर्यकोटिसमप्रभम् ।।१५५।।
ध्यायतो योगिनः सर्वमनोवृत्तिर्विनश्यति ।१५६।

dhyānenaiva samāyukto vyomni cātyantanirmale (152b)
sūryakoṭidyutidharaṃ nityoditamadokṣajam
hṛdayāmburuhāsīnaṃ dhyāyedvā viśvarūpiṇam (153)
ānekākāra khacitamanekavadanānvitam
anekabhujasaṃyuktamanekāyudhamaṇḍitam (154)
nānāvarṇadharaṃ devaṃ śāntamugramudāyudham
anekanayanākīrṇaṃ sūryakoṭisamaprabham (155)
dhyāyato yoginaḥ sarvamanovṛttirvinaśyati (156a)

Vocabulary

sarva-manaḥ-vṛttiḥ: every movement in the mind; *dhyāyataḥ yoginaḥ*: of the meditating yogin; *vinaśyati*: disappears; *samāyuktaḥ*: absorbed; *dhyānena*: in meditation; *atyanta-nirmale*: in the absolute purity; *vyomni*: of the ether; *nitya-uditam*: eternally sublime; *adokṣajam*: name of Viṣṇu; *dyuti-dharam*: shining with the radiance; *sūrya-koṭi*: crores of suns; *āsīnam*: seated on; *amburuha*: lotus; *hṛdaya*: of the heart; *vā dhyāyet*: or he should meditate; *viśva-rūpiṇam*: form of the universe; *ānekākāra*: many forms; *khacitam*: merged; *vadanān-vitam*: expanded into many faces; *aneka-bhuja-saṃyuktam*: joined with many hands; *aneka-āyudha-maṇḍitam*: adorned with many arms; *devam nānā-varṇa-dharam*: deva glowing with many colours; *śāntam-ugram*:

mild and fierce; *udāyudham*: with raised weapons; *ākīrṇam*: scattered with; *aneka-nayana*: many eyes; *samaprabham*: as dazzling as; *sūrya-koṭi*: crores of suns.

Translation

Every movement in the mind of the meditating yogin disappears [when he is] absorbed in meditation, in the absolute purity of the ether, on the eternally sublime Viṣṇu, shining with the radiance of crores of suns, seated on the lotus of the heart; or he should meditate on the form of the universe, [whose] many forms are merged, expanded into many faces, joined with many hands, adorned with many arms, a deva glowing with many colours, [both] mild and fierce with raised weapons, scattered with many eyes, as dazzling as crores of suns.

Commentary

The mind is completely clear and free from all thoughts when it is absorbed in Viṣṇu, the Supreme Consciousness whose light is brighter than a thousand suns, in *hṛdayākaśa*, the space where purity resides. Another practice is to meditate on the form of the universe which contains every form created by Brahma, the Creator.

Verses 156b to 165: Attaining Kaivalya

हृत्पुण्डरीकमध्यस्थं चैतन्यज्योतिरव्ययम् ।।१५६।।
कदम्बगोलकाकारं तुर्यातीतं परात्परम् ।
अनन्तमानन्दमयं चिन्मयं भास्करं विभुम् ।।१५७।।
निवातदीपसदृशमकृत्रिममणिप्रभम् ।
ध्यायतो योगिनस्तस्य मुक्तिः करतले स्थिता ।।१५८।।
विश्वरूपस्य देवस्य रूपं यत्किंचिदेव हि ।
स्थवीयः सूक्ष्ममन्यद्वा पश्यन्हृदयपङ्कजे ।।१५९।।
ध्यायतो योगिनो यस्तु साक्षादेव प्रकाशते ।
अणिमादिफलं चैव सुखेनैवोपजायते ।।१६०।।
जीवात्मनः परस्यापि यद्येवमुभयोरपि ।
अहमेव परंब्रह्म ब्रह्माहमिति संस्थितिः ।।१६१।।
समाधिः स तु विज्ञेयः सर्ववृत्तिविवर्जितः ।
ब्रह्म संपद्यते योगी न भूयः संसृतिं व्रजित् ।।१६२।।
एवं विशोध्य तत्त्वानि योगी निःस्पृहचेतसा ।
यथा निरिन्धनो वह्निः स्वयमेव प्रशाम्यति ।।१६३।।
ग्राह्याभावे मनःप्राणे निस्चयज्ञानसंयुतः ।
शुद्धसत्त्वे परे लीनो हीवः सैन्धवपिण्डवत् ।।१६४।।
मोहजालकसंघातं विश्वं पश्यति स्वप्नवत् ।
सुषुप्तिवद्यश्चरति स्वभावपरिनिश्चलः ।।१६५।।
निर्वाणपदमाश्रित्य योगी कैवल्यमश्नुत इत्युपनिषत् ।।

hṛtpuṇḍarīkamadhyastham caitanyajyotiravyayam (156b)
kadambagolakākāraṃ turyātītaṃ parātparam
anantamānandamayaṃ cinmayaṃ bhāskaraṃ vibhum (157)
nivātadīpasadṛśamakṛtrimamaṇiprabham
dhyāyato yoginastasya muktiḥ karatale sthitā (158)
viśvarūpasya devasya rūpaṃ yatkiṃcideva hi
sthavīyaḥ sūkṣmamanyadvā paśyanhṛdayapaṅkaje (159)
dhyāyato yogino yastu sākṣādeva prakāśate

aṇimādiphalaṃ caiva sukhenaivopajāyate (160)
jīvātmanaḥ parasyāpi yadyevamubhayorapi
ahameva paraṃbrahma brahmāhamiti saṃsthitiḥ (161)
samādhiḥ sa tu vijñeyaḥ sarvavṛttivivarjitaḥ
brahma saṃpadyate yogī na bhūyaḥ saṃsṛtiṃ vrajit (162)
evaṃ viśodhya tattvāni yogī niḥspṛhacetasā
yathā nirindhano vahniḥ svayameva praśāmyati (163)
grāhyābhāve manaḥprāṇe niścayajñānasaṃyutaḥ
śuddhasattve pare līno jīvaḥ saindhavapiṇḍavat (164)
mohajālakasaṃghātaṃ viśvaṃ paśyati svapnavat
suṣuptivadyaścarati svabhāvapariniścalaḥ (165)
nirvāṇapadamāśritya yogī kaivalyamaśnuta
ityupaniṣat

Vocabulary

muktiḥ: liberation; *tasya yoginaḥ*: of this yogin; *sthitā*: rests; *karatale*: in the palm of his hand; *dhyāyataḥ*: as he meditates on; *avyayam*: imperishable; *caitanya-jyotiḥ*: light of consciousness; *stham*: located in; *hṛt-puṇḍarīka-madhya*: middle of the lotus of the heart; *kadamba-golakākāram*: in the form of a cluster of kadamba flowers; *turyātītam*: beyond turya; *parātparam*: transcendent; *anantam*: endless; *ānanda-mayam*: full of bliss; *cit-mayam*: full of consciousness; *bhāskaram*: lustrous; *vibhum*: pervading; *dīpa-sadṛśam*: like a lamp; *nivāta*: sheltered from the wind; *prabham*: gleaming like; *akṛtrima-maṇi*: real jewel.
yoginaḥ yaḥ: yogin who; *paśyan*: seeing; *hṛdaya-paṅkaje*: in the sacred lotus in the heart; *sthavīyaḥ*: large; *sūkṣmam*: small; *anyat-vā*: or another; *yatkiṃcit*: whatever; *rūpam*: form; *devasya*: of the deva; *viśva-rūpasya*: of the form of the universe; *dhyāyataḥ*: meditates; *prakāśate*: it shines; *sākṣāt-eva*: before his very eyes; *ca sukhena*: and easily; *upajāyate*: it produces; *phalam*: fruit; *aṇima-ādi*: *aṇima* and others; *yadi saṃsthitiḥ*: if he is established; *ubhayoḥ*: in both; *jīvātmanaḥ api parasya*: individual and the supreme soul; *iti*: he can say; *aham eva*: I am indeed; *param-brahma*: Supreme Reality; *brahma-aham*: I am Brahma; *sa vijñeyaḥ samādhiḥ*: this is to

be known as *samādhi*; *sarvavṛttivivarjitaḥ*: devoid of all fluctuations; *yogī saṃpadyate brahma*: yogin is absorbed in Brahma; *na bhūyaḥ*: never again; *vrajit*: go; *saṃsṛtim*: course of mundane existence; *viśodhya evam tattvāni*: having thus purified the *tattvas*; *yogī cetasā*: yogin's mind; *niḥspṛha*: free from desire; *praśāmyati*: he becomes tranquil; *svayameva*: of his own accord; *yathā*: like; *vahniḥ*: fire; *nirindhanaḥ*: without fuel; *grāhya-abhāve*: in the absence of craving; *jīvaḥ*: *jīva*; *saṃyutaḥ*: contains; *niścaya-jñāna*: higher knowledge; *manaḥ-prāṇe*: in the mental prāṇa; *līnaḥ*: merges; *pare śuddha-sattve*: into transcendent pure essence; *piṇḍavat*: like a lump; *saindhava*: salt in the ocean; *paśyati*: sees; *viśvam*: universe; *saṃghātam*: combination; *moha-jālaka*: delusions and webs; *svapnavat*: as in a dream; *yogī yaḥ carati*: yogin who observes; *suṣuptivat*: as in sleep; *pariniścalaḥ*: firm in the recognition; *svabhāva*: his own true nature; *āśritya*: having reached; *nirvāṇa-padam*: state of nirvāṇa; *aśnuta kaivalyam*: attains *kaivalya*; *iti-upaniṣat*: thus ends the Upaniṣad.

Translation

The liberation of this yogin rests in the palm of his hand, as he meditates on the imperishable light of consciousness located in the middle of the lotus of the heart, in the form of a cluster of kadamba flowers, [which is] beyond turīya, transcendent, endless, full of bliss [and] consciousness, lustrous, pervading [all], like a lamp sheltered from the wind, gleaming like a real jewel.

The yogin who, seeing in the sacred lotus in the heart a large, a small or another whatever form of the deva, of the form of the universe, meditates [on it as] it shines before his very eyes, and easily produces the fruit [of] *aṇima* and others. If he is established in both the individual and the supreme soul, then he can say 'I am indeed the Supreme Reality, I am Brahman'. This is to be known as *samādhi*, devoid of all fluctuations.

The yogin is absorbed in Brahman, [and will] never again go [through] the course of mundane existence. Having thus purified the *tattvas*, the yogin's mind [is] free from desire. He becomes tranquil of his own accord, like a fire without fuel. In the absence of craving, the jīva, [which] contains higher knowledge in the mental prāṇa, merges into transcendent pure essence, like a lump [of] salt in the ocean [and] sees the universe as a combination [of] delusions and webs, as in a dream. The yogin who observes [this] as in sleep, firm in the recognition [of] his own true nature, having reached the state of *nirvāṇa*, attains *kaivalya.*

Thus ends the Upaniṣad.

Commentary

The heart is the abode of the *jīvātman*, the living soul. As described previously, mudrās help to channel the flow of prāṇa. In the palms of the hands are pressure points of meridians, pathways along which vital energy flows, to the heart. These pressure points are stimulated when the yogin is seated in meditation, hands in one of the hand mudrās.

The lotus is the subtle essence of the heart. It represents anāhata cakra, the psychic energy centre, located in the heart region The *kadamba* tree is associated with Lord Krishna. Its ball-shaped flowers are offered in temples. In *Kuṇḍalinī Tantra* it is said 'he who meditates on the heart lotus is foremost among yogis, pre-eminently wise and full of noble deeds. His senses are completely under control, and his mind can be engrossed in intense concentration'. [38]

The effects produced by meditation on the lotus of the heart are the eight major *siddhis* (powers): *aṇimā*, making the physical body smaller; *laghimā*: making the body lighter; *prāpti*: power to acquire [everything]; *prākāmya*: freedom of will; *mahimā*: increasing the size of the body; *īśitvam*: power to create and destroy; *vaśitva*: power of control; *garimā*: increasing the weight of the body. According to the

Yoga Tattwa Upanishad, these and other siddhis are obstacles on the path of yoga, because they are a distraction from the goal which is enlightenment while living in the physical body. The wise yogin will never show his powers or admit to having them, as others will use them for worldly purposes. [39]

Brahman is the pure, ever-expanding totality of consciousness. Brahma is the lord and creator of all, whose being is the essence of Brahman. When the yogin is firmly established in both the individual and the supreme soul, he activates and connects with the vibration of Brahman, the Supreme Consciousness, the source of all. Our true Self and Brahman have the same qualities. The wise person identifies with these qualities only, and not the gross body. He/she remains in the state of bliss of *Īśvara*, and, unaffected by external circumstances, affirms *aham brahmāsmi*, I am Brahman. Samādhi is the transcendental state of consciousness, in which all barriers and limitations of the conscious, subconscious, and unconscious are removed. In samādhi the consciousness is one indivisible field, total and complete.

Georg Feuerstein's invaluable *Encyclopedia of Yoga and Tantra* gives several definitions of *kaivalya*, the literal meaning of which is isolation. Kaivalya is defined as 'that which remains after the lower mind has been dissolved through yoga practice', and 'the light of aloneness (*kaivalya-jyotis*) which is motionless and full, resembling a flame in a windless place'. [40] 'The yogi now freed from the fourfold aims of life (*dharma, artha, kāma, mokṣa*). He is free from the gravitational pull of the three guṇas. He is a *guṇātītan.* This is the summit of yoga' [41]. Yoga Tattwa Upanishad defines the Supreme Seat as 'the indwelling, pure, undivided form of kaivalya, consisting of the form of sat-cit-ānanda' truth-pure consciousness-bliss beyond duality. [42]

APPENDICES

A. Notes

1. Frawley, David *Vedic Yoga: the Path of the Rishi* ((Lotus Press, Twin Lakes, Wisconsin 2014) p.234
2. Paramahamsa Niranjananda *Yoga Darshan* (Sri Panchdashnam Paramahamsa Alakh Bara 1993) p.34
3. Swami Satyasangananda Saraswati *Tattwa Shuddhi* (Bihar School of Yoga, Munger, Bihar, India 1993)
4. Paramahamsa Niranjananda *Yoga Darshan* (Sri Panchdashnam Paramahamsa Alakh Bara 1993)
5. Frawley, David *Vedic Yoga: the Path of the Rishi* ((Lotus Press, Twin Lakes, Wisconsin 2014) pp.110-111
6. Swami Satyasangananda Saraswati *Tattwa Shuddhi* (Bihar School of Yoga, Munger, Bihar India 1993) p.51
7. *ibidem* pp.46-47
8. Svoboda, Dr. Robert E. *Prakriti* (Lotus Press, Twin Lakes, Wisconsin 1998) p.73
9. *ibidem* p.13
10. Swami Satyananda Saraswati *Nine Principal Upanishads* (Yoga Publications Trust, Munger, Bihar India 2004) Mandukya Upaniṣad Verse 7, p.55
11. Feuerstein, Georg *The Yoga Tradition* (Hohm Press, Prescott, Arizona, 2001) p.217
12. Swami Satyadharma Saraswati *Yoga Darshana Upaniṣad* (2018) p.129 (translated by Ruth Perini)
13. *ibidem* p.80
14. *Bhagavad Gita* Srinivas Fine Arts Ltd (nightingale.co.in 2009) Ch.3, vs 19 p.173
15. Paramahamsa Niranjanananda *Karma Sannyasa & Dhyana* (Bihar School of Yoga, Munger, Bihar, India 1994) p.10
16. B.K.S. Iyengar *Light on the Yoga Sūtras of Patañjali* (Thorsons, Hammersmith, London, Great Britain 2002) *Sādhana Pāda* p.157 II.46 *sthirasukham āsanam*
17. Perini, Ruth *Shandilya Upanishad* (2020). This text has a more detailed commentary on *yama* and *niyama*.
18. *Bhagavad Gita* Srinivas Fine Arts Ltd (nightingale.co.in 2009) p.130 Vs.2:58

19. Feuerstein, Georg *The Philosophy, History and Literature of Yoga* (Yoga Research and Education Center, Manton, California USA 2003) p.636
20. Perini, Ruth *Shandilya Upanishad* (2020) pp52-54
21. *ibidem* Verse 11, 4th Section p59
22. B.K.S. Iyengar *Light on the Yoga Sūtras of Patañjali* (Thorsons, Hammersmith, London, Great Britain 2002) p.214
23. *ibidem*
24. Perini, Ruth *Shandilya Upanishad* (2020) pp 69-70
25. Swami Satyadharma Saraswati *Yoga Tattwa Upanishad* (2nd edition 2018) pp.66-67 (translated by Ruth Perini)
26. Feuerstein, Georg *The Encyclopedia of Yoga & Tantra* (Shambala Publications, Boulder, USA 2011) p.225
27. Swami Satyananda Saraswati *Kundalini Tantra* (Bihar School of Yoga, Munger, Bihar, India 1996) p.219
28. Swami Satyadharma Saraswati *Yoga Tattwa Upanishad* (2nd edition 2018) pp.87-88 Vs 51b-53a (translated by Ruth Perini)
29. Swami Satyananda Saraswati *Kundalini Tantra* (Bihar School of Yoga, Munger, Bihar, India 1996) pp.126, 129
30. Swami Satyananda Saraswati *Asana Pranayama Mudra Bandha* (Bihar Yoga Bharati, Munger, Bihar, India 1996) pp.446-448
31. Avalon, Arthur *The Serpent Power* (Dover Publications, New York, USA 1974) p.111
32. Feuerstein, Georg *The Encyclopedia of Yoga & Tantra* (Shambala Publications, Boulder, USA 2011) p.225
33. Swami Satyasangananda Saraswati *Tattwa Shuddhi* (Bihar School of Yoga, Munger, Bihar India 1993) p.51. Swami Satyadharma Saraswati *Yoga Tattwa Upanishad* (2nd edition 2018) p136, vs94b
34. *Śānti Parva,* ch. 352. The *Śānti Parva* by Vyāsa ('Book of Peace') is the twelfth of eighteen books of the Indian Epic *Mahabharata.* It traditionally has 3 sub-books and 365 chapters.
35. Paramahamsa Niranjanananda *Yoga Darshan* (Sri Panchdashnam Paramahamsa Alakh Bara 1993) p. 229
36. Swami Satyananda Saraswati *Asana Pranayama Mudra Bandha* (Bihar Yoga Bharati, Munger, Bihar, India 1996) pp.438-9

37. Feuerstein, Georg *The Encyclopedia of Yoga & Tantra* (Shambala Publications, Boulder, USA 2011) p.379
38. Swami Satyananda Saraswati *Kundalini Tantra* (Bihar School of Yoga, Munger, Bihar, India 1996) p.149
39. Swami Satyadharma Saraswati *Yoga Tattwa Upanishad* (2nd edition 2018) pp.115-6 (translated by Ruth Perini)
40. Feuerstein, Georg *The Encyclopedia of Yoga & Tantra* (Shambala Publications, Boulder, USA 2011) p.174
41. B.K.S.Iyengar *Light on the Yoga Sūtras of Patañjali* (Thorsons, Hammersmith, London, UK 2002) p243-4
42. Swami Satyadharma Saraswati *Yoga Tattwa Upanishad* (2nd edition 2018) Vs 17, p.43
43. Feuerstein, Kak, Frawley *In Search of the Cradle of Civilization* (Quest Books, Illinois, USA 2001) p.20

B. References

Avalon, Arthur *The Serpent Power* (Dover Publications, New York, USA 1974)

Ayyaṅgār, T.R.Ś. *The Yoga Upaniṣads* (The Adyar Library 1938)

Bhagavad Gita Srinivas Fine Arts Ltd (nightingale.co.in 2009)

Feuerstein, Georg, **Kak** Subash & **Frawley** David *In Search of the Cradle of Civilization* (Quest Books, Illinois USA 2001)

Feuerstein, Georg *The Encyclopedia of Yoga and Tantra* (Shambala Publications, Boulder, USA 2011)

Feuerstein, Georg *The Yoga-Sūtra of Patañjali* (Inner Traditions International, Vermont USA 1979)

Feuerstein, Georg *The Yoga Tradition* (Hohm Press, Prescott, Arizona, 2001)

Frawley, David *Gods, Sages and Kings* (Passage Press, Salt Lake City, Utah USA 1991)

Frawley, David *Vedic Yoga: The Path of the Rishi* ((Lotus Press, Twin Lakes, Wisconsin 2014)

B.K.S. Iyengar *Light on the Yoga Sūtras of Patañjali* (Thorsons, Hammersmith, London, Great Britain 2002)

Joshi Bimali Trivedi *112 Upaniṣads* (Parimal Publications, Delhi India 2007)

Paramahamsa Niranjanananda *Karma Sannyasa & Dhyana* (Yoga Publications Trust, Munger, Bihar, India 1994)

Paramahamsa Niranjanananda *Yoga Darshan* (Sri Panchdashnam Paramahamsa Alakh Bara 1993)

Paramahamsa Niranjanananda *Dharana Darshan* (Sri Panchdashnam Paramahamsa Alakh Bara 1993)

Perini, Ruth *Shandilya Upanishad* (2020)

Svoboda, Dr. Robert E. *Prakriti* (Lotus Press, Twin Lakes, Wisconsin 1998)

Swami Satyadharma Saraswati *Yoga Chudamani Upanishad* (Yoga Publications Trust, Munger, Bihar, India 2003)

Swami Satyadharma Saraswati *Yoga Darshana Upaniṣad* (2018)

Swami Satyadharma Saraswati *Yoga Tattwa Upanishad* (2nd edition 2018)

Swami Satyananda Saraswati *Asana Pranayama Mudra Bandha* (Bihar Yoga Bharati, Munger, Bihar, India 1996)

Swami Satyananda Saraswati *Kundalini Tantra* (Bihar School of Yoga, Munger, Bihar, India 1996)

Swami Satyananda Saraswati *Mandukya Upaniṣad: Nine Principal Upanishads* (Yoga Publications Trust, Munger, Bihar India 2004)

Swami Satyananda Saraswati *Nine Principal Upanishads* (Yoga Publications Trust, Bihar 1975

Swami Satyasangananda Saraswati *Tattwa Shuddhi* (Bihar School of Yoga, Munger, Bihar, India 1993)

Swami Yogakanti *Sanskrit Glossary of Yogic Terms* (Yoga Publications Trust, Munger, Bihar, India 2007)

C. Pronunciation Guide

a	nut
ā	father
i	bit
ī	knee
u	hook
ū	sue
ṛ	hurt
e	net
ai	time
o	got
au	house
ṃ	hum
ḥ	h + preceding vowel
k	paprika
kh	ink horn
g	ago
gh	big hut
ṅ	anger
c	chat
ch	much harm
j	jog
jh	raj house
ñ	engine
ṭ	borscht
ṭh	borscht home
ḍ	fresh dill
ḍh	flushed heart
ṇ	rainy
t	tarp
th	scout hall
d	modern
dh	mud hut

n	banal
p	papa
ph	top half
b	maybe
bh	mob hall
m	chroma
y	young
r	merit
l	alas
v	lava
ś	shin
ṣ	sunshine
h	hut

D. Sanskrit Text

त्रिशिखी ब्राह्मणोपनिषद्

।।शान्तिपाठः।।

ॐ पूर्णमदः पूर्णमिदम् पूर्नात् पूर्णमुदच्यते ।
पूर्णस्य पूर्णमादाय पूर्णमेव अवशिष्यते ।।
ॐ शान्तिः शान्तिः शान्तिः ।।

।।ब्राह्मणम् १।।
त्रिशिखी ब्राह्मण आदित्यलोकं जगाम तं गत्वोवाच ।
भगवन् किं देहः किं प्राणः किं कारणं किमात्मा ।।१।।
स होवाच सर्वमिदं शिव एव विचानीहि ।
किंतु नित्यः शुद्धो निरञ्जनो विभुरद्वयानन्दः शिव एकः स्वेन भासेदं
सर्वं दृष्ट्वा तप्तायः पिण्डवदेकं भिन्नवदवभासते ।
तद्भासकं किमिति चेदुच्यते ।
सच्छब्दवाच्यमविद्याशबलं ब्रह्म ।।२।।

ब्रह्मणोऽव्यक्तम् । अव्यक्तान्महत् । महतोऽहंकारः ।
अहंकारात्पाञ्चतन्मात्राणि । पञ्चतन्मात्रेभ्यः पञ्चमहाभूतानि ।
पञ्चमहाभूतेभ्योऽखिलं जगत् ।।३।।
तदखिलं किमिति । भूतविकारविभागादिरिति ।
एकस्मिन्पिण्डे कथं भूतविकारविभाग इति ।
तत्तत्कार्यकारणभेदरूपेणांशतत्त्ववाचकवाच्यस्थानभेदविषयदेवताकोशभेदविभागा भवन्ति ।।४।।

अथाकाशोऽन्तःकरणमनोबुद्धिचित्ताहंकाराः ।
वायुः समानोदानव्यानापानप्राणाः ।
वह्निः श्रोत्रत्वक्चक्षुर्जिह्वाघ्राणानि ।
आपः शब्दस्पर्शरूपरसगन्धाः ।
पृथिवी वाक्पाणिपादपायूपस्थाः ।।५।।

ज्ञानसंकल्पनिश्चयानुसंधानाभिमाना आकाशकार्यान्तःकरणविषयाः ।
समीकरणोन्नयनग्रहणश्रवणोच्छ्वासा वायुकार्यप्राणादिविषयाः ।
शब्दस्पर्शरूपरसगान्धा अग्निकार्यज्ञानेन्द्रियविषया अबाश्रिताः ।
वानादानगमनविसर्गानन्दाः पृथिवीकार्यकर्मेन्द्रिय विषयाः ।
कर्मज्ञानेन्द्रियविषयेषु प्राणतन्मात्रविषया अन्तर्भूतः ।
मनोबुद्ध्योश्चित्ताहंकारौ चान्तर्भूतौ ।।६।।

अवकाशविधूतदर्शनपिण्डीकरणधारणाः सूक्ष्मतमा जैवतन्मात्रविषयाः ।।७।।

एवं द्वादशाङ्गानि आध्यात्मिकान्याधिभौतिकान्याधिदैविकानि ।
अत्र निशाकरचतुर्मुखदिग्वातार्कवरुणाश्व्यग्नीन्द्रेपेन्द्रप्रजापतियमा इत्यक्षाधिदेवतारूपैर्द्वादशनाड्यन्तःप्रवृत्ताः प्राणा एवाङ्गानि अंगज्ञानं तदेव ज्ञातेति ।।८।।

अथ व्योमानिलानलजलपृथिव्योनानां पञ्चीकरणमिति ।
ज्ञातृत्वं समानयोगेन श्रोत्रद्वारा शब्दगुणो वागधिष्ठित आकाशे तिष्ठति आकाशस्तिष्ठति ।

मनो व्यानयोगेन त्वग्द्वारा स्पर्शगुणः पाण्यधिष्ठितो वायौ तिष्ठति वायुस्तिष्ठति ।

बुद्धिरुदानयोगेन चक्षुर्द्वारा रूपगुणः पादाधिष्ठितोऽग्नौ तिष्ठत्यग्निस्तिष्ठति ।

चित्तमपानयोगेन जिह्वाद्वारा रसगुण उपस्थाधिष्ठितोऽप्सु तिष्ठत्यापस्तिष्ठन्ति ।

अहंकारः प्राणयोगेन घ्राणद्वारा गन्धगुणो गुदाधिष्ठितः पृथिव्यां तिष्ठति पृथिवी तिष्ठति य एवं वेद ।।९।।

मन्त्र २

अत्रैते श्लोका भवन्ति ।।

पृथग्भूते षोडश कलाः स्वार्धभागान्परान्क्रमात् ।
अन्तःकरणव्यानाक्षिरसपायुनभः क्रमात् ।।१।।
मुख्यात्पूर्वोत्तरैर्भूतेभूते चतुश्चतुः ।
पूर्वमाकाशमाश्रित्य पृथिव्यादिषु संस्थिताः ।।२।।
एवंशो ह्यभूतस्मात्तेभ्यश्चांशो ह्यभूत्तथा ।।३।।
तस्मादन्योन्यमाश्रित्य ह्योतं प्रोतमनुक्रमात् ।४।

पञ्चभूतमयी भूमिः सा चेतनसमन्विता ।।४।।
तत ओषधयोऽन्नं च ततः पिण्डाश्चतुर्विधाः ।
रसासृङ्मांसमेदोऽस्थिमज्जाशुक्राणि धातवः ।।५।।

केचित्तद्योगतः पिण्डा भूतेभ्यः संभवाः क्वचित् ।

तस्मिनन्नमयः पिण्डो नाभिमण्डलसंस्थितः ।।६।।
अस्य मध्येऽस्ति हृदयं सनालं पद्मकोशवत् ।
सत्त्वानतर्वार्तिनो देवाः कर्त्रहंकारचेतनाः ।।७।।
अस्य बीजं तमःपिण्डं मोहरूपं जडं घनम् ।
वर्तते कण्ठमाश्रित्य मिश्रीभूतमिदं जगत् ।।८।।

प्रत्यगानन्दरूपात्मा मूर्ध्नि स्थाने परे पदे ।
अनन्तशक्तिसंयुक्तो जगद्रूपेण भासते ।।९।।

सर्वत्र वर्तते जाग्रत्स्वप्नं जाग्रति वर्तते ।
सुषुप्तं च तुरीयं च नान्यावस्थासु कुत्रचित् ।।१०।।
सर्वदेशेष्वनुस्यूतश्चतूरूपः शिवात्मकः ।
यथा महाफले सर्वे रसाः सर्वप्रवर्तकाः ।।११।।

तथैवान्नमये कोशे कोशास्तिष्ठन्ति जान्तरे ।
यथा कोशस्तथा जीवो यथा जीवस्तथा शिवः ।।१२।।
सविकारस्तथा जीवो निर्विकारस्तथा शिवः ।
कोशास्तस्य विकारास्ते ह्यवस्थासु प्रवर्तकाः ।।१३।।

यथा रसाशये फेनं मथनादेव जायते ।
मनोनिर्मथनादेव विकल्पा बहवस्तथा ।।१४।।
कर्मणा वर्तते कर्मो तत्त्यागाच्छान्तिमाप्नुयात् ।
अयने दक्षिणे प्राप्ते प्रपञ्चाभिमुखं गतः ।।१५।।

अहकाराभिगानेन जीवः स्याद्धि सदाशिवः ।
स चाविवेकप्रकृतिसङ्गत्या तत्र मुह्यते ।।१६।।
नानायोनिशतं गत्वा शेतेऽसौ वासनावशात् ।
विमोक्षात्संचरत्येव मत्स्यः कूलद्वयं यथा ।।१७।।
ततः कालवशादेव ह्यात्मज्ञानविवेकतः
उत्तराभिमुखो भूत्वा स्थानात्स्थानान्तरं क्रमात् ।।१८।।

मूर्धन्याधायात्मनः प्राणान्योगाभ्यासं स्थितश्चरन् ।
योगात्संजायते ज्ञानं ज्ञानाद्योगः प्रवर्तते ।।१९।।

योगज्ञानपरो नित्यं स योगी न प्रणश्यति ।
विकारस्थं शिवं पश्येद्विकारश्च शिवे न तु ॥२०॥
योगप्रकाशक्रं योगैर्ध्यायेच्चानन्यभावनः ।
योगज्ञाने न विद्येते तस्य भावो न सिध्यति ॥२१॥
तस्मादभ्यासयोगेन मनः प्राणान्निरोधयेत् ।
योगी निशितधारेण क्षुरेणैव निकृन्तयेत् ॥२२॥
शिखा ज्ञानमयी वृत्तिर्य माद्यष्टाङ्गसाधनैः ।
ज्ञानयोगः कर्मयोग इति योगो द्विधा मतः ॥२३॥

क्रियायोगमथेदानीं शृणु ब्राह्मणसत्तम् ।
अव्याकुलस्य चित्तस्य बन्धनं विषये क्वचित् ॥२४॥
यत्संयोगो द्विजश्रेष्ठ स च द्वैविध्यमश्नुते ।
कर्म कर्तव्यमित्येव विहितेष्वेव कर्मसु ॥२५॥
बन्धनं मनसा नित्यं कर्मयोगः स उच्यते ।
यत्तु चित्तस्य सततमर्थे श्रेयसि बन्धनम् ॥२६॥

ज्ञानयोगः स विज्ञेयः सर्वसिद्धिकरः शिवः ।
यस्योक्तलक्षणे योगे द्विविधेऽप्यव्ययं मनः ॥२७॥
स याति परमं श्रेयो मोक्षलक्षणमञ्जसा ।२८।

देहेन्द्रियेषु वैराग्यं यम इत्युच्यते बुधैः ॥२८॥
अनुरक्तिः परे तत्त्वे सततं नियमः स्मृतः ।
सर्ववस्तून्युदासीनभावमासनमुत्तमम् ॥२९॥
जगत्सर्वमिदं मिथ्याप्रतीतिः प्राणसंयमः ।
चित्तस्यान्तर्मुखभावः प्रत्याहारस्तु सत्तम ॥३०॥
चित्तस्य निश्चलीभावो धारणा धारणां विदुः ।
सोऽहं चिन्मात्रमेवेति चिन्तनं ध्यानमुच्यते ॥३१॥
ध्यानस्य विस्मृतिः सम्यक्समाधिरभिधीयते ।३२।

अहिंसा सत्यमस्तेयं ब्रह्मचर्यं दयार्ज्वम् ।।३२।।
क्षमा धृतिर्मिताहारः शौचं चेति यमा दश ।
तपः सन्तुष्टिरास्तिक्यं दानमाराधनं हरेः ।।३३।।
वेदान्तश्रवणं चैव ह्रीर्मतिश्च जपो व्रतम् । इति ।३४।

आसानानि तदङ्गानि स्वस्तिकादीनि वै द्विज ।।३४।।
वर्ण्यन्ते स्वस्तिकं पादतलयोरुभयोरपि ।
पूर्वोत्तरे जानुनी द्वे कृत्वासनमुदीरितम् ।।३५।।
सव्ये दक्षिणगुल्फं तु पृष्ठपार्श्वे नियोजयेत् ।
दक्षिणेऽपि तथा सव्यं गोमुखं गोमुखं यथा ।।३६।।
एकं चरणमन्यस्मिन्नूरावारोपि निश्चलः ।
आस्ते यदिदमेनोघ्नं वीरासनमुदीरितम् ।।३७।।

गुदं नियम्य गुल्फाभ्यां व्युत्क्रमेण समाहितः ।
योगासनं भवेदेतदिति योगविदो विदुः ।।३८।।
ऊर्ध्वोरुपरि वै धत्ते यदा पादतले उभे ।
पद्मासनं भवेदेतत्सर्वव्याधिविषापहम् ।।३९।।
पद्मासनं सुसंस्थाप्य तदङ्गुष्ठद्वयं पुनः ।
व्युत्क्रमेणैव हस्ताभ्यां बद्धपद्मासनं भवेत् ।।४०।।

पद्मासनं सुसंस्थाप्य जानूर्वोरन्तरे करौ ।
निवेश्य भूमावातिष्ठेद्व्योमस्थः कुक्कुटासनः ।।४१।।
कुक्कुटासनबन्धस्थो दोर्भ्यां संबध्य कन्धरम् ।
शेते कूर्मवदुत्तान एतदुत्तानकूर्मकम् ।।४२।।
पादाङ्गुष्ठौ तु पाणिभ्यां गृहीत्वा श्रवणावधि ।
धनुराकर्णकाकृष्टं धनुरासनमीरितम् ।।४३।।

सीवनीं गुल्फदेशाभ्यां निपीड्य व्युत्क्रमेण तु ।
प्रसार्य जानुनोर्हस्तावासनं सिंहरूपकम् ॥४४॥
गुल्फौ च वृषणस्याधाः सीविन्युभयपार्श्वयोः ।
निवेश्य पादौ हस्ताभ्यां बध्वा भद्रासनं भवेत् ॥४५॥
सीवनीपार्श्वमुभयं गुल्फाभ्यां व्युत्क्रमेण तु ।
निपीड्यासनमेतच्च मुक्तासनमुदीरितम् ॥४६॥

अवष्टब्य धरां सम्यक्तलाभ्यां हस्तयोर्द्वयोः ।
कूर्परौ नाभिपार्श्वे तु स्थापयित्वा मयूरवत् ॥४७॥
समुन्नतशिरः पादं मयूरासनमिष्यते ।
वामोरुमूले दक्षाङ्घ्रिं जान्वोर्वेष्टिपाणिना ॥४८॥
वामेन वामाङ्गुष्ठं तु गृहीतं मत्स्यपीठकम् ।
योनिं वामेन संपीड्य मेढ्राद्दुपरि दक्षिनम् ॥४९॥

वामोरुमूले दक्षाङ्घ्रिं जान्वोर्वेष्टिपाणिना ॥४८॥
वामेन वामाङ्गुष्ठं तु गृहीतं मत्स्यपीठकम् ।
योनिं वामेन संपीड्य मेढ्राद्दुपरि दक्षिनम् ॥४९॥
ऋजुकायः समासीनः सिद्धासनमुदीरितम् ।
प्रसार्य भुवि पादौ तु दोर्भ्यामङ्गुष्ठमादरात् ॥५०॥
जानूपरि ललाटं तु पश्चिमोत्तानमुच्यते ।
येन प्रकारेण सुखं धार्यं च जायते ॥५१॥
तत्सुखासनमित्युक्तमशक्रस्तत्समाचरेत् ।
आसनं विजितं येन जितं तेन जगत्त्रयम् ॥५२॥

यमैश्च नियमैश्चैव आसनैश्च सुसंयतः ।
नाडीशुद्धिं च कृत्वादौ प्राणायामं समाचरेत् ॥५३॥
देहमानं स्वाङ्गुलिभिः षण्णवत्यङ्गुलायतम् ।

प्राणः शरीरादधिको द्वादशाङ्गुलमानतः ।।५४।।
देहस्थमनिलं देहसमुद्भूतेन वह्निना ।
न्यूनं समं वा योगेन कुर्वन्ब्रह्विवदिष्यते ।।५५।।

देहमध्ये शिखिस्थानं तप्तजाम्बूनदप्रभम् ।
त्रिकोणं द्विपदामन्यच्चतुरस्त्रं चतुष्पदम् ।।५६।।
वृत्तं विहङ्गमानां तु सदस्त्रं सर्पजन्मनाम् ।
अष्टास्त्रं स्वेदजानां तु तस्मिन्दीपवदुज्ज्वलम् ।।५७।।

कन्दस्थानं मनुष्याणां देहमध्यं नवाङ्गुलम् ।
चतुरङ्गुलमुत्सेधं चतुरङ्गुलमायतम् ।।५८।।
अण्डाकृति तिरश्चां च द्विजानां च चतुष्पदाम् ।
तुन्दमध्यं तदिष्टं वै तन्मध्यं नाभिरिष्यते ।।५९।।

तत्र चक्रं द्वादशारं तेषु विष्णवादिमूर्तयः ।
अहं तत्र स्थितश्चक्रं भ्रामयामि स्वमायया ।।६०।
अरेषु भ्रमते जीवः क्रमेण द्विजसत्तम ।
तन्तुपञ्चरमध्यस्था यथा भ्रमति लूतिका ।।६१।।
प्राणाविरूढश्चरति जीवस्तेन विना न हि
तस्योर्ध्वे कुण्डलीस्थानं नाभिस्तिर्यकशोर्ध्वतः ।।६२।।

अष्टप्रकृतिरूपा सा चाष्टधा कुण्डलीकृता ।
यथावद्वायुसारं च ज्वलनादि च नित्यशः ।।६३।।
परितः कन्दपार्श्वे तु निरुध्यैव सदा स्थिता ।
मुखेनैव समावेष्ट्य ब्रह्मरन्ध्रमुखं तथा ।।६४।।
योगकालेन मरुता साग्निना बोधिता सती ।
स्फुरिता हृदयाकाशे नागरूपा महोज्ज्वला ।।६५।।

अपानाद्द्व्यङ्गुलादूर्ध्वमधो मेढ्रस्य तावता ।
देहमध्यं मनुष्याणां हृन्मध्यं तु चतुष्पदाम् ।।६६।।
इतरेषां तुन्दमध्ये नानानाडीसमावृतम् ।
चतुष्प्रकारद्व्ययुते देहमध्ये सुषुम्नया ।।६७।।
कन्दमध्ये स्थिता नाडी सुषुम्ना सुप्रतिष्ठिता ।
पद्मसूत्रप्रतीकाशा ऋजुरूर्ध्वप्रवर्तिती ।।६८।।
ब्रह्मणो विवरं यावद्विद्युदाभामनालकम् ।
वैष्णवी ब्रह्मनाडी च निर्वाणप्राप्तिपद्धतिः ।।६९।।

इडा च पिङ्गला चैव तस्याः सव्येतरे स्थिते ।
इडा समुत्थिता कन्दाद्वामनासापुटावधिः ।।७०।।
पिङ्गला चोत्थिता तस्माद्दक्षनासापुटावधिः ।
गान्धारी हस्तिजिह्वा च द्वे चान्ये नाडिके स्थिते ।।७१।।
पुरतः पृष्ठस्तस्य वामेतरदृशौ प्रति ।
पूषायशस्विनीनाड्यौ तस्मादेव समुत्थिते ।।७२।।
सव्येतरश्रुत्यवधि पायुमूलादलम्बुसा ।
अधोगता शुभा नाडी मेढ्रान्तावधिरायता ।।७३।।
पादाङ्गुष्ठावधिः कन्दादधोयाता च कौशिकी ।
दशप्रकारभूतास्ताः कथिताः कन्दसंभवाः ।।७४।।
तन्मूला बहवो नाड्यः स्थूलसूक्ष्माश्च नाडिकाः ।
द्वासप्ततिसहस्राणि स्थूलाः सूक्ष्माश्च नाड्यः ।।७५।।
संख्यातुं नैव शक्यन्ते स्थूलमूलाः ।
यथाश्वत्थदले सूक्ष्मा स्थूलाश्च विततास्तथा ।।७६।।
प्राणापानौ समानश्च उदानो व्यान एव च ।
नागः कूर्मश्च कृकरो देवदत्तो धनंजयः ।।७७।।
चरन्ति दशनाडीषु दश प्रानादिवायवः ।
प्रानादिपञ्चकं तेषु प्रधानं तत्र च द्वयम् ।।७८।।

प्राण एवाथवा ज्येष्ठो जीवात्मानं बिभर्ति यः ।
आस्यनासिकयोर्मध्यं हृदयं नाभिमण्डलम् ।।७९।।
पादाङ्गुष्ठमिति प्राणस्थानानि द्विजसत्तम् ।
अपानश्चरति ब्रह्मन्गुदमेढ्रोरुजानुषु ।।८०।।
समानः सर्वगात्रेषु सर्वव्यापी व्यवस्थितः ।
उदानः सर्वसन्धिस्थः पादयोर्हस्तयोरपि ।।८१।।
व्यानः श्रोत्रोरुकट्यां च गुल्फस्कन्धगलेषु च ।
नागादिवायवः पञ्च त्वगस्थ्यादिषु संस्थिताः ।।८२।।

तुन्दस्थजलमन्नं च तसादीनि समीकृतम् ।
तुन्दमध्यगतः प्राणस्तानि कुर्यात्पृथक्पृथक् ।।८३।।
इत्यादिचेष्टनं प्राणः करोति च पृथक् स्थितम्
अपानवायुर्मूत्रादेः करोति च विसर्जनम् ।।८४।।
प्राणापानादिचेष्टादि क्रियते व्यानवायुना ।
उज्जीर्यते शरीरस्थमुदानेन नभस्वता ।।८५।।
पोषणादिशरीरस्य समानः कुरुते सदा ।
उद्गारादिक्रियो नागः कूर्मोऽक्षादिनिमीलनः ।।८६।।
कृकरः क्षुधयोः कर्ता दत्तो निद्रादिकर्मकृत् ।
कृतगात्रस्य शोभादेर्धनंजय उदाहृतः ।।८७।।
नाडीभेदं मरुद्भेदं मरुतां स्थानमेव च ।
चेष्टाश्च विविधास्तेषां ज्ञात्वैव द्विजसत्तम् ।।८८।।
शुद्धौ यतेत नाडीनां पूर्वोक्तज्ञानसंयुतः ।८९।

विविक्तदेशमासाद्य सर्वसंबन्धवर्जितः ।।८९।।
योगाङ्गद्रव्यसंपूर्णं तत्र दारुमये शुभे ।
आसने कल्पिते दर्भकुशकृष्णाजिनादिभिः ।।९०।।
तावदासनमुत्सेधे तावद्द्वयसमायते ।

उपविश्यासनं सम्यक्स्वस्तिकादि यथारुचि ।।९१।।

बद्ध्वा प्रागासनं ऋजुकायः समाहितः ।
नासाग्रयस्तनयनो दन्तैर्दन्तानसंस्पृशन् ।।९२।।
रसनां तालुनि न्यस्य स्वस्थचित्तो निरामयः ।
आकुञ्चितशिरः किंचिन्निबध्नन्योगमुद्रया ।।९३।।
हस्तौ यथोक्तविधिना प्राणायामं समाचरेत् ।
रेचनं पूरणं वायोः शोधनं रेचनं तथा ।।९४।।

चतुर्भिः क्लेशनं वायोः प्राणायाम उदीर्यते ।
हस्तेन दक्षिणेनैव पीडयेन्नासिकापुटम् ।।९५।।
शनैः शनैरथ बहिहः प्रत्रिपेत्पिङ्गलानिलम् ।
इडया वायुमापूर्य ब्रह्मन्षोडशमात्रया ।।९६।।
पूरितं कुम्भयेत्पश्चाच्चतुःषष्ट्या तु मात्रया ।
द्वात्रिंशन्मात्रया सम्यग्रेचयेत्पिङ्गलानिलम् ।।९७।।
एवं पुनः पुनः कार्यं व्युत्क्रमानुक्रमेण तु
संपूर्णकुम्भवद्देहं कुम्भयेन्मातरिश्चना ।।९८।।
पूरणान्नाड्यः सर्वाः पूर्यन्ते मातरिश्चना ।
एवं कृते सति ब्रह्मंश्चरन्ति दश वायवः ।।९९।।
हृदयाम्भोरुहं चापि व्याकोचं भवति स्फुटम् ।
तत्र पश्येत्परात्मानं वासुदेवमकल्मषम् ।।१००।।
प्रातर्माध्यन्दिने सायमर्धरात्रे च कुम्भकान् ।
शनैरशीतिपर्यन्तं चतुर्वारं समभ्यसेत् ।।१०१।।
एकाहमात्रं कुर्वाणः सर्वपापैः प्रमुच्यते ।
संवत्सरत्रयादूर्ध्वं प्राणायामपरो नरः ।।१०२।।
योगसिद्धो भवेद्योगी वायुजिद्विजितेन्द्रियः ।
अल्पाशी स्वल्पाशी स्वल्पनिद्रश्च तेजस्वी बलवान्भवेत् ।।१०३।।
अपमृत्युमतिक्रम्य दीर्घमायुरवाप्नुयात् ।१०४।
कम्पनं वपुषो यस्य प्राणायामेषु मध्यमः ।

उत्थानं वपुषो यस्य स उत्तम उदाहृतः ॥१०५॥
अधमे व्याधिपापानां नाशः स्यान्मध्यमे पुनः।
पापतोगमहाव्याधिनाशः स्यादुत्तमे पुनः ॥१०६॥

अल्पमूत्रोऽल्पविष्ठश्च लघुदेहो मिताशनः ।
पट्विन्द्रियः पटुमतिः कालत्रयविदात्मवान् ॥१०७॥
रेचकं पूरकं मुक्त्वा कुम्भिकरणमेव यः ।
करोति त्रिषु कालेषु नैव तस्यास्ति दुर्लभम् ॥१०८॥
नाभिकन्दे च नासाग्रे पादाङ्गुष्ठे च यत्नवान् ।
धारयेन्मनसा प्राणान्सन्ध्याकालेषु वा सदा ॥१०९॥
सर्वरोगैर्विनिर्मुक्तो जीवेद्योगी गतक्लमः ।
कुक्षिरोगविनाशः स्यान्नाभिकन्देषु धारणात् ॥११०॥

नासग्रे धारणाद्दीर्घमायुः सयाद्देहलाघवम् ।
ब्राह्मे मुहूर्ते संप्राप्ते वायुमाकृष्य जिह्वया ॥१११॥
पिबतस्त्रिषु मासेषु वाक्षिद्धिर्महती भवेत् ।
अभ्यासतश्च षण्मासान्महारोगविनाशनम् ॥११२॥
यत्र यत्र धृता वायुरङ्गे रोगादिदूषिते ।
धारणादेव मरुतस्तत्तदारोग्यमश्नुते ॥११३॥

मनसा धारणादेव पवनो धारितो भवेत् ।
मनसः स्थापने हेतुरुच्यते द्विजपुङ्गव ॥११४॥
करणानि समाहृत्य विषयेभ्यः समाहितः ।
अपानमूर्ध्वमाकृष्येदुदरोपरि धारयेत् ॥११५॥
बध्नन्कराभ्यां श्रोत्रादिकरणानि यथातथम् ।
युन्जास्य यथोक्तेन वर्त्मना स्ववशं मनः ॥११६॥
मनोवशात्प्राणवायुः स्ववशे स्थाप्यते सदा ।

नासिकापुटयोः प्राणः पर्यायेण प्रवर्तते ।।११७।।

तिस्रश्च नाडिकास्तासु स यावन्तं चरत्ययम् ।
शङ्खिनीविवरे याम्ये प्राणः प्राणभृतां सताम् ।।११८।।
तावन्तं च पुनः कालं सौम्ये चरति संततम् ।
इत्थं क्रमेण चरता वायुना वायुजिन्नरः ।।११९।।
अहश्च रात्रिं पक्षं च मासमृत्वयनादिकम् ।
अन्तर्मुखे विजानीजात्कालभेदं समाहितः ।।१२०।।

अङ्गुष्ठादिस्वावयवस्फुरणादर्शनैरपि ।
अरिष्टैर्जीवितस्यापि जानीयात्क्षयमात्मनः ।।१२१।।
ज्ञात्वा यतेत कैवल्यप्राप्तये योगवित्तमः ।
पादाङ्गुष्ठे कराङ्गुष्ठे स्फुरणं यस्य स्रुति ।।१२२।।
तस्य संवत्सरादूर्ध्वं जीवितस्य क्षयो भवेत् ।
मणिबन्धे तथा गुल्फे स्फुरणं यस्य नश्यति ।।१२३।।
षण्मासावधिरेतस्य जीवितस्य स्थितिर्भवेत् ।
कूर्परे स्फुरणं यस्य तस्य त्रैमासिकी स्थितिः ।।१२४।।
कुक्षिमुहनपार्श्वे च स्फुरणानुपलम्भने ।
मासावधिर्जीवितस्य तदर्धस्य तु दर्शने ।।१२५।।
आश्रिते हठरद्वारे दिनानि दश जीवितम् ।
ज्योतिः खद्योतवद्यस्य तदर्धं तस्य जीवितम् ।।१२६।।

जिह्वाग्रादर्शने त्रीणि दिनानि स्थितिरात्मनः ।
ज्वालाय दर्शने मृतुर्द्विदिने भवति ध्रुवम् ।।१२७।।
एवमादीन्यरिष्टानि दृष्टायुः क्षयकारणम् ।
निःश्रेयसाय युञ्जीत जपध्यानपरायणः ।।१२८।।
मनसा परमात्मानं ध्यात्वा तद्रूपतामियात् ।१२९।

यद्यष्टादशभेदेषु मर्मस्थानेषु धारणम् ।।१२९।।
स्थानात्स्थानं समाकृष्य प्रत्याहारः स उच्यते ।
पादाङ्गुष्ठं तथा गुल्फं जङ्घामध्यं तथैव च ।।१३०।।
मध्यमूर्वोश्च मूलं च पायुर्हृदयमेव च ।
मेहनं देहमध्यं च नाभिं च गलकूर्परम् ।।१३१।।
तालुमूलं च मूलं च घ्राणस्याक्ष्णोश्च मण्डलम् ।
भ्रुवोर्मध्यं ललाटं च मूलमूर्ध्वं च जानुनी ।।१३२।।
मूलं च करयोर्मूलं महान्त्येतानि वै द्विज ।
पञ्चभूतमये देहे भूतेष्वेतेषु पञ्चसु ।।१३३।।
मनसा धारणं यत्तद्युक्तस्य च यमादिभिः ।
धारणा सा च संसारसागरोत्तारणम् ।।१३४।।

आजानुपादपर्यन्तं पृथिवीस्थानमिष्यते ।
पित्तला चतुरस्रा च वसुधा वज्रलाञ्छता ।।१३५।।
स्मर्तव्या पञ्चघटिकास्त्रारोप्य प्रभञ्जनम् ।
आजानुकटिपर्यन्तमपां स्थानं प्रकीर्तितम् ।।१३६।।
अर्धचन्द्रसमाकारं श्वेतमर्जुनलाच्छितम् ।
स्मर्तव्यमम्भःश्वसनमारोप्य दश नाडिकाः ।।१३७।
आदेहमध्यकट्यन्तमग्निस्थानमुदाहृतम् ।
तत्र सिन्धूरवर्णोऽग्निर्ज्वलनं दश पञ्च च ।।१३८।।
स्मर्तव्या नाडिकाः प्राणं कृत्वा कुम्भे तथेरिताम् ।
नाभेरुपारि नासान्तं वायुस्थानं तु तत्र वै ।।१३९।।
वेदिकाकारवद्धूम्रो बलवान्भूतमारुतः ।
स्मर्तव्यः कुम्भकेनैव प्राणमारोपय मारुतम् ।।१४०।।
घटिकाविंशतिस्तस्माद् घ्राणाद्ब्रह्मबिलावधि ।
व्योमस्थानं नभस्तत्र बिन्नाञ्जनसमप्रभम् ।।१४१।।

व्योम्नि नारुतमारोप्य कुम्भकेनैव यत्नवान् ।१४२।
पृथिव्यंशे तु देहस्य चतुर्बाहुं किरीटिनम् ।।१४२।।
अनिरुद्धं हरिं योगी यतेत भवमुक्तये ।
अबंशे पूरयेद्योगी नारायणमुदग्रधीः ।।१४३।।
प्रद्युम्नमग्नौ वाय्वंशे संकर्षणमतः परम् ।
व्योमांशे परमात्मानं वासुदेवं सदा स्मरेत् ।।१४४।।
आचिरादेव तत्प्राप्तिर्युञ्जानस्य न संशयः ।१४५।

बद्धवा योगासनं पूर्वं हृद्देशे हृदयाञ्जलिः ।।१४५।।
नासाग्रन्यस्तनयनो जिह्वां कृत्वा च तालुनि ।
दन्तैर्दन्तानसंस्पृश्य उर्ध्वकायः समाहितः ।।१४६।।
संयमेच्चेन्द्रियग्राममात्मबुद्ध्या विशुद्धया ।
चिन्तनं वासुदेवस्य परस्य परमात्मनः ।।१४७।।
स्वरूपव्याप्तरूपस्य ध्यानं कैवल्यसिद्धिदम् ।
याममात्रं वासुदेवं दिन्तयेत्कुम्भकेन यः ।।१४८।।
सप्तजन्मार्जितं पापं तस्य नश्यति योगिनः ।१४९।

नाभिकन्दात्समारभ्य यावद्धृदयगोचरम् ।।१४९।।
जाग्रद्वृत्तिं विजानीयात्कण्ठस्थं स्वप्नवर्तनम् ।
सुषुप्तं तालुमध्यस्थं तुर्यं भ्रूमध्यसंस्थितम् ।।१५०।।
तुर्यातीतं परं ब्रह्म ब्रह्मरन्द्रे तु लक्षयेत् ।
जाग्रद्वृत्तिं समारभ्य यावद्ब्रह्मबिलान्तरम् ।।१५१।।
तत्रात्मायं तुरीयस्य तुर्यन्ते विष्णुरुच्यते ।१५२।
ध्यानेनैव समायुक्तो व्योम्नि चात्यन्तनिर्मले ।।१५२।।
सूर्यकोटिद्युतिधरं नित्योदितमदोक्षजम् ।
हृदयाम्बुरुहासीनं ध्यायेद्वा विश्वरूपिणम् ।।१५३।।

हृत्पुण्डरीकमध्यस्थं चैतन्यज्योतिरव्ययम् ।।१५६।।
कदम्बगोलकाकारं तुर्यातीतं परात्परम् ।
अनन्तमानन्दमयं चिन्मयं भास्करं विभुम् ।।१५७।।
निवातदीपसदृशमकृत्रिममणिप्रभम् ।
ध्यायतो योगिनस्तस्य मुक्तिः करतले स्थिता ।।१५८।।
विश्वरूपस्य देवस्य रूपं यत्किंचिदेव हि ।
स्थवीयः सूक्ष्ममन्यद्वा पश्यन्हृदयपङ्कजे ।।१५९।।
ध्यायतो योगिनो यस्तु साक्षादेव प्रकाशते ।
अणिमादिफलं चैव सुखेनैवोपजायते ।।१६०।।
जीवात्मनः परस्यापि यद्येवमुभयोरपि ।
अहमेव परंब्रह्म ब्रह्माहमिति संस्थितिः ।।१६१।।
समाधिः स तु विज्ञेयः सर्ववृत्तिविवर्जितः ।
ब्रह्म संपद्यते योगी न भूयः संसृतिं व्रजित् ।।१६२।।
एवं विशोध्य तत्त्वानि योगी निःस्पृहचेतसा ।
यथा निरिन्धनो वह्निः स्वयमेव प्रशाम्यति ।।१६३।।
ग्राह्याभावे मनःप्राणे निस्चयज्ञानसंयुतः ।
शुद्धसत्त्वे परे लीनो हीवः सैन्धवपिण्डवत् ।।१६४।।
मोहजालकसंघातं विश्वं पश्यति स्वप्नवत् ।
सुषुप्तिवद्यश्चरति स्वभावपरिनिश्चलः ।।१६५।।
निर्वाणपदमाश्रित्य योगी कैवल्यमश्नुत इत्युपनिषत् ।।

निर्वाणपदमाश्रित्य योगी कैवल्यमश्नुत इत्युपनिषत् ।।

E. Continuous Translation

Opening Invocation

Om, that is full, this is full. From the full comes the full.
If the full is taken from the full, only the full remains.

First Text

1 and 2.

The *brāhmaṇa* with three tufts of hair went to the world of the Sun. Having arrived, he asked Him: "O Lord! What is the body? What is the breath? What is the cause? What is the soul?"

He replied: "All this indeed leads only from the form of Śiva, the one Śiva [who is] eternal, faultless, pure, [whose] bliss [is] supreme and non-dual. Seeing all this with His own light, He shines forth in different forms like a mass [of] molten iron. If one asks from where is this luminescence, [it is] Brahman [who is] replete with the knowledge [of] the true sound [attained through] restraining speech.

3 and 4.

From Brahman [came] the unmanifest; from the unmanifest [came] the greater mind; from the greater mind [came] the individual form; from the individual form [came] the five senses; from the five senses [came] the five elements; from the five elements [came] the entire world.

What is this entire [world]? At the beginning [there were] divisions [and] changes in the elements. How were there divisions and changes in the elements in each body of matter? The parts of the elements are made in the form [of] different causes. They are the different divisions of topics, deities and sheaths, [and] the distinction [between] speaker and speech.

5.
Now ether [includes] the *antaḥ karaṇa, manas, buddhi, citta* and *ahaṃkāra.* Air [includes] *samāna, udāna, vyāna, apāna* and *prāṇa.* Fire [includes] ears, skin, eyes, tongue and nose. Water [includes] sound, touch, appearance, taste and smell. Earth [includes] speech, hands, feet, anus and genital organs.

6.
Knowledge, purpose, determination, inquiry [and] desire [are in] the scope of the mind [and] functions of the ether element. Uniting, elevating, holding, hearing [and] exhaling [are] in the scope of the prāṇas [and] functions of the air element. Sound, touch, appearance, taste [and] smell [are] in the scope of the organs of perception [and] functions of the fire element. They are related to the element of water. Speech, receiving, moving, voiding [and] pleasure [are] in the scope of the organs of action [and] functions of the earth element.

The domains of prāṇa and *tanmātra* are contained in the domains of [both] the organs of perception and action. Citta and ahaṃkāra are both contained in manas and buddhi.

7.
The most subtle parts [of] the personal tanmātras [are] space, spreading, seeing, combining [and] stability.

8.
Thus, the twelve parts [include] those which relate to the spiritual Self, the physical [and] the Divine. Here, it is said, the moon, the four-faced one, the directions, wind, sun, ocean, Aśvini, Agni, Indra, Upendra, Prajāpati [and] Yama move as components of prāṇa in the twelve *nāḍīs* in the forms [of] presiding deities [of] the senses. It is said [that whoever] knows this [has] knowledge of the Self.

9.
Now the synthesis of the five different elements, ether, wind, fire, water and earth, is explained. Here is [the element of] ether: inner knowledge together with samāna, [having] the quality of sound [which comes] through the ear [and] is regulated by the vocal cords, abides in the ether. Here is [the element of] air: the mind together with vyāna, [having] the quality of touch through the skin [and] connected with the hands, abides in the air. Here is [the element of] fire: the discerning mind together with udāna, [having] the quality of sight through the eyes [and] dependent on the feet, abides in the fire. Here is [the element of] water: memory together with apāna, [having] the quality of taste through the tongue [and] connected with the genitals, abides in water. Here is [the element of] earth: the individual self together with prāṇa, [having] the quality of smell through the nose, connected with the anus, abides in earth. Whoever knows thus [is a yogin].

Second Text

1 to 4a.
In [each] separate element the sixteen parts [are formed] by degrees [into] two equal parts, [and] by degrees [into] mind, wind, eyes, essence, anus [and] nose. First and foremost, in each element, preceding and following, [there are] four [parts], [then] four [again], starting with ether [and] concluding with earth and the others. That is why [each] section [that is] made from them, [the other] sections are made in that manner. Dependent on one another, [each] is fixed by this method.

4b and 5.
The world, consisting of the five elements, possesses consciousness, food possessing medicine, and then four kinds [of] forms, [and] the constituents [of] fluid, blood, flesh, fat, bone, marrow [and] sexual fluid.

6 to 8.

[Because of] this apparent combination [of elements], [there are] then possibilities [of] crystals [made] from the elements. The form made of food remains here in the region of the navel. The heart has a stalk like the calyx of a lotus in its middle, [and] the gods whose consciousness [is] the destroyer [of] the ego dwell in harmony [there]. Its seed exists [in] the throat as 'material particles of potential energy'[9] consisting of delusion [and] a mass [of] ignorance, dependent on this world of mixed elements.

9.

The *ātman* [is] the form of Supreme Bliss situated at the crown [of] the head. Endowed with the infinite *śakti,* it shines in the highest position through its worldly form.

10 and 11.

The waking [state] is everywhere. Dreaming is in the waking [state]. Deep sleep and the state beyond are nowhere in the other states. Just as tastes are produced in every great fruit, [so] the four states pervaded by the essence of Śiva are strung together in all the states.

12 and 13.

Likewise, *koṣas* are produced within *annamaya koṣa*, just as the koṣa is the individual soul, so the individual soul [is] Śiva. Thus, the individual [is] changeable, [but] Śiva [is] unchangeable. The koṣas have differences which are produced in the states of existence.

14 and 15.

Just as foam is produced by churning liquid in a receptacle, similarly by churning the mind many false notions [arise]. Through action *karma* exists. Through renunciation one obtains peace. If one arrives by the southern way, one faces the visible world.

16 to 18.

Indeed, [one who has reached] Sadāśiva may become a jīva through the arrogance of ego, and can go astray by mixing with people [who] lack discrimination. Having gone through many hundreds [of] wombs, that [person] remains helpless with desires, just like a fish moving [between] the two banks of a river away from liberation. Then, through the rule of time, the wise person, having faced north [and going] step by step from place to place, [gains] knowledge of the ātman.

19 to 23.

[When] the mind has been placed firmly at the crown of the head, [and] the vital energies moved [with] the practice of yoga, [then] through yoga wisdom arises, and through wisdom yoga ensues. [When] both yoga and jñāna [are] constant, the yogin does not perish. He sees Śiva where there are defects, but not defects in Śiva. Through the practices of yoga, he should meditate on the light of yoga and with no other thought. If he does not have yoga and jñāna, his contemplation will not succeed. Thus, by the practice of yoga, the yogin should control the mind with the force of vital energy as if he was cutting with the sharp blade of a knife. With the regular practice [of] the eightfold path, beginning with yama, the modifications of the mind are transformed [into] the flame of jñāna. Thus yoga is regarded as twofold, the yoga of knowledge [and] the yoga of action.

24 to 28a.

O most venerable Brāhmaṇa, listen now to [the meaning of] kriyā yoga. Now in its subject matter [there is] restraint of the confused mind. O excellent Twice-born, whatever combination [one uses], one can reach the twofold state, when duty [and] action are done as prescribed [in the scriptures]. Karma yoga, it is said, always [has] control of the mind. By means of this continuous control, [there is] benefit for the mind. Whoever knows jñāna yoga, has all the powers of Śiva. Thus it is said if the aim [is] the twofold yoga, then the mind [is] imperishable. The accomplished one, [whose] aim is liberation, instantly goes to the Absolute.

28b to 32a.

Thus it is said by the wise that *yama* [is] detachment from the sense organs of the body. *Niyama* is described as continuous devotion to the transcendental essence. The attitude [of] non-attachment [to] all things [is] the supreme *āsana*. [In] the control of vital airs [one understands] the false belief [in] this whole world. Now *pratyāhāra* is first introversion of the mind. Fixed concentration on the mind is known as *dhāraṇā*. Pure intelligence is really the thought 'That I am'. This is called *dhyāna*. Loss of memory [of the previous states] in dhyāna is duly expressed as *samādhi*.

32b to 34a.

The ten yamas are non-violence, truth, honesty, celibacy, kindness, straightforwardness, patience, steadiness, diet and cleanliness. [The niyamas] are self-discipline, complete contentment, theism, generosity, worship of the Divine, listening to the Vedas, remorse, faith, mantra repetition and resolution.

34b to 40.

O Brāhmaṇa, then the branches of *āsana, svastika* and others, are described. Placing both soles of the feet in front of and above the two knees is called *svastikāsana*. Now placing the right ankle on the left beside the back, and similarly the left on the right [is] *gomukha*, the cow-face [pose]. If one is firmly seated, each foot on the opposite thigh, this is called *vīrāsana*. [When] the contracted anus has been pressed by both ankles, by turning [them] up, this is *yogāsana*. So say the wise who know yoga. When both soles of the feet are placed upwards on the thighs, this is *padmāsana*. This [is] an antidote to all disease. Positioned again in padmāsana, the two big toes turned up by the hands, this is *baddha-padmāsana*.

41 to 46.

Positioned in padmāsana, putting [the hands] inside the knees, placing [them] on the ground [and] locked in *kukkuṭāsana*, one should hold kukkuṭāsana in the air. Having bound the neck with the shoulders, resting spread out like a tortoise, this [is] the stretched-out tortoise [pose], *kūrmāsana*. Pulling the feet up to the ears with the hands, the legs spread out [and] drawn up like a bow, is called *dhanurāsana*. Pressing the genitals with parts of the upturned ankles, extending the posture with hands on the knees, [is] the form of the lion, *siṃhāsana*. Placing the ankles below the testicles on both sides of the buttocks [and] holding the feet with the hands, is *bhadrāsana*. Pressing both sides of the genitals with the ankles turned up, this āsana is called *muktāsana*.

47 to 52.

Grasping [and] holding the soles of the feet together with two hands, [and] now placing the elbows near the navel like a peacock, head [and] feet raised, one moves into *mayūrāsana*. Knees bent, [place] the right foot with the left hand on top [of] the left thigh, now grasping the left big toe, [this is] *matsyāsana*. Pressing the vulva with the left [foot], the right [foot] above the genitals, seated [with] a straight body, is called *siddhāsana*. Legs stretched out on the floor, carefully [hold] the big toes by the forearms, then the forehead above the knees. [This] is called *paścimottānāsana*. A comfortable and stable [posture] is called *sukhāsana*. [It is for those who are] unable [to] practise [an āsana] in whichever way. Whoever has conquered āsana, has therefore conquered the three worlds.

53 to 55.

Having first [gained] good control by means of the yamas, niyamas and āsanas and begun purification of the nāḍīs, one should practise *prāṇāyāma*.The height of the [human] body [is] ninety-six fingers long [when measured] by one's own fingers. The prāṇa extends more than twelve fingers from the body. Making the wind located in the body less or equal to the fire produced in the body through yoga, one gains knowledge of Brahman.

56 and 57:

The region of fire, [which is] triangular [and as] radiant [as] molten gold, [is] in the middle of the two-footed [being]. In four-footed [beings], [it is] quadrangular. In birds [it is] round, hexagonal in snakes [and] octagonal in those produced by sweat.

58 to 62:

The place of the *kanda* is nine digits in the centre of the human body, [and is] luminous as a lamp. [It is] four digits in height [and] four digits in width. It is oval-shaped in both those with two and those with four legs, and across the middle of the navel. Indeed the navel is considered [to be] its centre. There is a cakra with twelve spokes. In them are the deities of Viṣṇu and others. I, through my own power, cause the cakra located there to move about. The jīva whirls among its spokes, o excellent Brāhmaṇa, in the same way as the spider wanders about in the midst of the five-spoked cobweb. The jīva moves by the flowing prāṇa, without which it cannot [exist]. Now over it is the place of the kuṇḍalinī horizontally above the navel.

63 to 65.

She [kuṇḍalinī has] the form [of] the eight elements of nature, and making eightfold coils, which having constantly controlled both the energy of the vital air and the roaring of the fire all around {and] beside the kanda, she remains ever thus, covering with her mouth the mouth of the *brahmarandhra*. At the time of yoga, [when] she is illuminated by air [and] fire, a great blaze in the form of the serpent breaks forth in the heart space.

66 to 69.
Two fingers upwards from apāna [at maṇipura] to [two fingers] below the genital organ [is] the middle of the body in humans. The heart centre [is the middle of the body] in the four-footed. In the rest [it is] in the centre of the abdomen enveloped by many nāḍīs. In the centre of the body [with] the four times twenty thousand nāḍīs is suṣumnā nāḍī firmly established in the centre of the kanda, *Brahmanāḍī*, luminous [as] lightning, moves straight upwards like the stalk of a lotus to the Brahma opening right up to the stalkless divine power of Viṣṇu and the way to reach final liberation.

70 to 76.
Iḍā and *piṅgalā* [nāḍīs] are on its left and right. Iḍā rises from the kanda right up to the cavity [of] the left nostril, and piṅgalā extends from it right up to the cavity [of] the right nostril. Both *gāndhārī* and *hastijihvā* are two other nāḍīs. [They are] at its front [and] back up to both eyes. The *pūṣā* and *yaśasvinī* nāḍīs rise up to the left and right ears from the base of the anus. *Alambusā*, the auspicious nāḍī, goes down [and] extends right to the end of the penis. *Kauśikī* goes down from the kanda right to the big toe. These ten types of channels are said to originate from the kanda. From that root [are] many gross and subtle nāḍīs. [There are] seventy-two thousand gross and subtle nāḍīs. The subtle roots cannot even be counted, just as the small and large leaves [of] the holy fig tree spread far beyond.

77 to 82.
The ten vital airs, beginning with prāṇa, [are] *prāṇa apāna samāna, udāna, vyāna,* and also *nāga, kūrma, kṛkara*, *devadatta* and *dhanaṃjaya* move about in ten nāḍīs. The first five [are] the major [ones] in these [nāḍīs] and of those the first two prāṇas [are those], which it is said, support the individual soul. The centre of the mouth and nose, the heart, navel [and] big toes are the abodes of prāṇa, o Excellent Twice-born one! Apāna moves in the anus, genitals, thighs

and knees, o Brāhmaṇa! Samāna spreads throughout all the limbs. Udāna is located in all the joints of feet and hands too. Vyāna is in the ears, hips and waist, and in the ankles, shoulders and neck. The five winds of Nāga and others are located in the skin and bones.

83 to 89a.

The water, food and other fluids in the belly are assimilated, [and] prāṇa, having gone to the centre of the belly, separates them from each other. Thus the prāṇa performs these [functions], remaining separate. The apāna wind discharges urine etc. The actions of prāṇa and apāna etc are made by the vyāna wind and stimulated by the udāna wind in the body. Samāna always performs the nourishing etc of the body. The action [of] nāga [is] belching etc, [and of] kūrma [is] shutting the eyes etc. Kṛkara causes hunger, devadatta controls sleep etc [and] dhanaṃjaya is said to bring lustre to the body. Having thus known, o Brāhmaṇa, the differences among the various nāḍīs and vital airs, [and] the position of the vital airs and their diverse functions, and absorbed the knowledge mentioned above, one should do purification of the nāḍīs.

89b to 91.

Having settled in a secluded place, renounced all associations, and, having acquired materials there [for] the practice of yoga, one should make a comfortable wooden seat with *darbha kuśa* and black deerskin etc. [and] sit correctly in the āsana of one's choice, such as svastikāsana etc, both in an upright and extended posture.

92 to 94.

Being fixed in āsana as before, the body erect [and] steady, the gaze placed at the nosetip, not touching the teeth with the teeth, the tongue placed on the palate, free from thoughts, abiding in the Self, the head inclined slightly, holding the hands in *yoga mudrā*, one should practise *prāṇāyāma* by the prescribed method, inhaling [and] exhaling. Therefore exhalation [is] purification of the vital airs.

95 to 101.

It is called prāṇāyāma through the four activities of the breath. One should press the purified nostril with the right hand. Having inhaled through the left nostril sixteen *mātrās*, one should now gradually exhale through the right nostril, o Brahman. After inhaling one should retain [the breath] for sixty-four mātrās, then exhale through the right nostril for exactly thirty-two mātrās. Thus [this practice] is to be done in sequence [and] in the reverse order. The inhaled wind is retained like a pot [in] the body.

O Brahman, when inflated all the nāḍīs are filled with vital wind. When [this] is being done thus, the ten winds move about. The lotus heart becomes fully expanded and also clear. One can see there the pure Vāsudeva [as] the Supreme Soul. One should practise breath retention four times [a day], in the morning, at midday, in the evening and at midnight, gradually up to eighty [times].

102 to 104a.

One is freed from all sins by doing [this practice] for one whole day. The person absorbed in prāṇāyāma upwards from three years becomes perfected in yoga. The yogin, having controlled the winds [and] conquered the senses, eating little, enjoying little and sleeping little, becomes radiant and powerful. He achieves long life by overcoming sudden death.

104b to 110.

Now it is said [that] the prāṇāyāma, the production of which [is] perspiration [is] the [most] inferior, while the prāṇāyāmas the characteristic of which [is] shivering [is] medium [and] that which has the characteristic [of] rising [is] the best. The destruction of disease and sins is in the inferior [and] again in the medium [effect]. The destruction of sins, sickness and plagues is the best [effect], as well as little urine, little excrement, a light body and a frugal diet.

The wise person, [who has] sharp senses [and] a keen mind, has knowledge of the three stages. Whoever does the practice [of] breath retention, freed from inhalation [and] exhalation, can without difficulty attain within the three *kālas*. The aspirant should hold the prāṇas by means of the mind at the knot at the navel, the nosetip and the big toes always at the times of dawn, noon and dusk. Delivered from all diseases, the yogin lives refreshed. Disease of the abdomen is destroyed through concentration on the knot at the navel.

111 to 113.

Through concentration on the nosetip, there is long life [and] lightness of the body. Having drawn in the air through the tongue [and] drunk[it], when *brahmamuhūrta* is reached, one has great power of speech within three months, and with regular practice for six months, [there is] destruction [of] major disease. Wherever there is contamination by disease etc, then by fixing one's concentration on that limb, the vital air has mastery over the diseased area.

114 to 117.

Thus by concentration through the mind the wind is held. It is said the means for firmly establishing the activities about this matter [is] in the region of the mind, o esteemed Brāhmaṇa! One should draw upwards the *apāna* [and] hold [it] above the abdomen. Having precisely performed through this method the binding [of] the ears and other [sense organs] with the hands, one is said [to have] a self-controlled mind. By command of the mind, the vital air is always kept under its control. Through [this] way the prāṇa activates the purification of the nostrils.

118 to 120.

[There are] three nāḍīs. In these this prāṇa, full of continual vital energy, moves as much through the right cave [of] the nerve as it again continually moves through the left. So the person [who] controls the vital air by the regular flow of wind for a day and night, fortnight, month and other proper times, [whose mind is] steadfast, turned inwards, understands the division of time.

121 to 129a.

By the disappearance of the vibration of the yogin's vital airs in the thumbs and other [limbs] as well as forebodings about his life, he knows the end of his self. Knowing this, [whoever has] the highest knowledge of yoga should reach kaivalya. The end of his life will be in a year or more when the vibration in the feet and hands fades away. Similarly when the vibration in the wrist and ankle disappears, there will remain a limit of six months of his life. His stay [in the world] lasts three months when the vibration in the elbow [disappears]. If no evidence [of any] vibration is seen near the abdomen and genitals, then within a month, half his life [is gone]. If there is [no vibration] at the entrance to the stomach, [there remains] ten days [of] life, then this half-life is a light illuminating the sky. When the tip of the tongue is not seen, the remainder of the self [is] three days. When a flame is seen, death is definite in two days. Having seen such signs [of] destruction, he should prepare himself for the ultimate bliss by intent practice [of] japa and meditation. Having meditated on the Supreme Self through the mind, he attains the state of that form.

129b to 134.

If [there is] the holding [of the vital air] on the eighteen different seats of *marman*, withdrawing from seat to seat is called *pratyāhāra*. Thus the big toes, the ankles and in the same manner the middle of the shanks, the middle of the thighs and their base, the anus and the heart, the genitals, the middle of the body, the navel, the throat, elbows, the root of the palate and the root of the nose, the region of the eyes, the eyebrow centre, the base and top [of] the forehead, the root [of] the knees and of the hands, these, o Twice-Born, [are the seats] in the five great elements. Once concentration through the mind on the five elements in the body [is] established by the *yamas* and other [limbs of yoga], then [there is] *dhāraṇā*, the cause of the crossing [of] the ocean [of] worldly existence.

135 to 145a.

The seat of earth goes [from] the feet right up to the knees. Earth, yellow and square, the sign of the diamond, [is] to be meditated on for five *ghaṭikās* (two hours), having been filled with vital air. The seat of water is said [to be from] the knees right up to the waist. Water like the [shape of] the crescent moon, [whose] mark [is] silver and white, should be contemplated on for ten *nāḍikās*, the wind having been inhaled [there]. From the middle of the body down to the hip is called the place of fire. There, the prāṇa having been retained, the vermilion-coloured blazing fire should be meditated on for fifteen nāḍikās, so it is said.

The seat of air [is] there from above the navel up to the nose. The strong element of air, smoke-coloured, with the shape of an altar, should thus be meditated on for twenty ghaṭikās (eight hours), the prāṇa having been inhaled with retention at [the seat of] vital air. From the nose up to the crown of the head [is] the seat of ether. The ether there [is] as bright as pounded antimony. Having inhaled the vital air with retention in ether, [one should hold it there] with great effort.

In the part of the body [which is] the earth element, the yogin should endeavour to free himself from mundane existence [by meditating on] Aniruddha [and] four-armed Viṣṇu adorned with a crown. The yogin should inhale deeply, [and] always meditate, his mind exalted, on Nārāyaṇa in the region of the water element, Pradyumna in the fire element, Samkarsana in the region of the air element, [and] next the Supreme Self, Vāsudeva, in the region of the ether element. [There is] no doubt that the yogin will attain in a short time.

145b to 149a.
Firmly settled in yogāsana as before, the hṛdayāñjali mudrā in the region of the heart, eyes fixed on the nosetip, and having placed the tongue on the palate, not touching teeth with teeth, body upright, steadfast, he should restrain all sense organs, purifying [the mind and] attaining knowledge of the Self. Reflecting on the Supreme Vāsudeva, the Transcendent Self, meditating on [Him] whose form has pervaded one's own form [he has] the power of final liberation. That yogin, who reflects on Vāsudeva for one yāma with breath restraint, will erase the sins [of] seven previous births.

149b to 152a.
[The place] beginning from the knot of the navel up to the region of the heart [is] the waking state. From there the state of dreaming is in the area of the throat. Deep sleep [is] in the middle of the palate [and] *turīya*, the fourth state, is fixed at the eyebrow centre. One perceives what is beyond turīya, the Supreme Brahman, in the *brahmarandra*, beginning from the waking state up to the crevice of Brahman. There [is] the seer of turīya, the end of which is said [to be] Viṣṇu.

152b to 156a.
Every movement in the mind of the meditating yogin disappears [when he is] absorbed in meditation, in the absolute purity of the ether, on the eternally sublime Viṣṇu, shining with the radiance of crores of suns, seated on the lotus of the heart; or he should meditate on the form of the universe, [whose] many forms are merged, expanded into many faces, joined with many hands, adorned with many arms, a deva glowing with many colours, [both] mild and fierce with raised weapons, scattered with many eyes, as dazzling as crores of suns.

156b to 165.
The liberation of this yogin rests in the palm of his hand, as he meditates on the imperishable light of consciousness

located in the middle of the lotus of the heart, in the form of a cluster of kadamba flowers, [which is] beyond turīya, transcendent, endless, full of bliss [and] consciousness, lustrous, pervading [all], like a lamp sheltered from the wind, gleaming like a real jewel.

The yogin who, seeing in the sacred lotus in the heart a large, a small or another whatever form of the deva, of the form of the universe, meditates [on it as] it shines before his very eyes, and easily produces the fruit [of] aṇima and others. If he is established in both the individual and the supreme soul, then he can say 'I am indeed the Supreme Reality, I am Brahman'. This is to be known as samādhi, devoid of all fluctuations. The yogin is absorbed in Brahman, [and will] never again go [through] the course of mundane existence. Having thus purified the tattvas, the yogin's mind [is] free from desire. He becomes tranquil of his own accord, like a fire without fuel. In the absence of craving, the jīva, [which] contains higher knowledge in the mental prāṇa, merges into transcendent pure essence, like a lump [of] salt in the ocean [and] sees the universe as a combination [of] delusions and webs, as in a dream. The yogin who observes [this] as in sleep, firm in the recognition [of] his own true nature, having reached the state of *nirvāṇa*, attains *kaivalya.*

Thus ends the Upaniṣad.

F. Swami Satyadharma

On 12th June 2019 on the Central Coast of New South Wales, Australia, our beloved Swami Satyadharma left her body. It was on the day of Ganga Dussehra, celebrating the descent to earth of the goddess Ganga, Ganga the mother providing nourishment to all her children.

Dedications in her commentaries on the Yoga Upanishads have been to all spiritual aspirants. Swami Satyadharma's life was dedicated for over forty years to providing spiritual nourishment and bringing the light of yoga to all those who attended her programs throughout the world.

Swami Satyadharma was born in 1946 to a middle-class family in Connecticut, USA. She was the youngest of three and lived surrounded by nature and animals. She recognised the spiritual energy of nature, and was never attracted to big cities.

In search of purpose and spiritual guidance she travelled for years throughout Europe, Africa and Asia, where she met many enlightened masters. She spent two years in Nepal studying with Tibetan Buddhist lamas. She was an accomplished musician of the flute and guitar, and spent two years at the University of Bengal studying the sitar. In Java, Indonesia she first studied batik, and then took part in a meditation program in one of the Javanese mystical schools. Her teacher was a mahasiddha who was 'breathtaking, awe-inspiring, transformative'. He specifically singled her out and said 'you have a future if you go and study earnestly, and after a long time you will attain an elevated consciousness as a yoga teacher, and you'll spend the later part of your life travelling internationally, and you'll teach the highest level yoga teachings'. She was directed by the master to go to Mungher, Bihar, India, where she would meet a great teacher, Swami Satyananda, a disciple of Swami Sivananda.

There she stayed for thirty-five years. At the age of 28, she was initiated by Swami Satyananda into *pūrṇa sannyasa* (full renunciation), a Dashnami order connected with the Advaita Vedanta tradition established by Adi Shankaracharya to protect, preserve and propagate spiritual knowledge. She absorbed the teachings and worked hard for the ashram for the first twenty years she spent there.

Then she edited books written by Swami Satyananda and, under his guidance, travelled the world teaching a range of different spiritual courses on the Yogic Scriptures. And teach she did in Australia, USA, Canada, India, Nepal, Tibet, China, Japan, Korea, Columbia, Greece, Germany, Hungary, Bulgaria, France, Italy, Indonesia, New Zealand. In all those countries she was invited to come back time and time again. She had a great ability to teach. Her vast knowledge of the ancient scriptures was amazing. It just flowed from her. When she taught it was like she stepped into another zone, where she spoke with profound insight. That is why, if Swami Satyadharma was running a course, people would sign up regardless of the topic. Her deep understanding of yoga was reflected in the numerous topics she taught.

Her later years were devoted to writing commentaries on the Yoga Upanishads, including *Yoga Tattwa*, *Yoga Darshana*, *Yoga Kundali*, *Nadabindu* and *Dhyanabindu* Upanishads.

Swami Satyadharma's Programs, Retreats &Lectures Programs

Awakening Kundalini, Meditations from the Tantras, Dancing with Divine, Atma Darshan, Intuition, Guru Tattwa, Shiva Sutras, Mantra Yantra and Mandala, Ashram Life, Sadhana, Chakra Meditation, Spiritual Life.

***Deepening Sadhana* Retreats**

Kriya Yoga, Tattwa Shuddhi, Chakra Shuddhi, Prana Vidya and Mahavidya Sadhana.

Lectures

During the years she lived in Australia, she gave many satsangs and lectures to students enrolled in Yogic Studies courses. Topics included Origins of Yoga, Samkhya Tantra & Vedanta, Yoga Sutras, Koshas, Chakras, Gunas, Bhagavad Gita, SWAN Theory, Raja Yoga, Gyan Yoga, Bhakti Yoga, Karma Yoga, Hatha Yoga, Upanishads, Pranava, Shiva Shakti, Mantra & Nada, Mantra Yoga, Nada Yoga, Mudra & Bandha,Shatkarmas, Kundalini Yoga, Swara Yoga, Prana & Pranayama, Pratyahara, Theory & Practice of Antar Mouna, Yoga Psychology, Yoga Philosophy, Yoga in India, Yoga Ecology, Yoga History, Path of the Rishis, Yamas & Niyamas, Yoga & Religion, Meditation, Yoga Nidra, Addiction,Purpose in Life, Grief, Body-Mind Therapy, Opening the Heart, Perception, Models of Mind, Mind & Consciousness, Mind Management and Living Consciously.

I was privileged to have worked with Swami Satyadharma for nine years. Her unlimited love and teachings will live on well into the future.

Om Tat Sat

Srimukti

G. Author's Note

I started working with Swami Satyadharma early in 2010, collating teachings on Bhakti Yoga, Rāja Yoga and Jñāna Yoga. I then had a yoga studio in Sydney, Australia, where I would invite senior teachers to give weekend programs. Swami Satyadharma had agreed to give a program on *Prāṇa Prāṇāyama Prāṇa Vidyā*. As usual with her programs, it was booked out well in advance. In 2011 she gave a program on *Managing the Mind through Meditation* and in 2014 *Yoga of the Heart* at a time when she was very supportive to me as my husband was ill in hospital.

Our working relationship and friendship developed over the nine years I worked with her on the teachings project and later as translator of the Yoga Upanishads on which she wrote commentaries. She had asked me what I was going to do with the Sanskrit I had studied. "Look for something to translate, I suppose," I said. "I've got something for you to translate: the Yoga Upanishads, there are only twenty-one of them," she said as if the matter had been settled. The project was unique because there were no other published commentaries on the Yoga Upanishads, except for *Chudamani Upanishad* which she'd completed in Bihar in 2003. Later she told me she had made a *sankalpa* before she moved to Australia that she would find a translator here.

Together we we collaborated on the *Yoga Tattwa, Yoga Darshana*, *Yoga Kundali, Nadabindu* and *Dhyanabindu*

Upanishads. Wherever we were, at her home, on a bushwalk or at a beach, we would have long talks about the work we were doing together. She wanted us to work on *Shandilya Upanishad* next, so I started the translation and commentary in August 2019 and it was published on her birthday 26th June 2020. I commenced work on *Triśikhī-Brāhmaṇopaniṣad* in August 2020, and it has now been published.

For many years I was a teacher of yoga and meditation. Already a linguist, having graduated in French, Italian and Japanese from the Universities of Sydney and Queensland, Australia, I undertook four years of studies in Sanskrit at the Australian National University (ANU) with Dr McComas Taylor. I was invited to join the Golden Key International Society for outstanding academic achievement, having gained High Distinctions throughout my Sanskrit studies.

Ruth Perini
(Srimukti) 15th
November 2021
yoga.upanishads@yahoo.com

www.ingramcontent.com/pod-product-compliance
Lightning Source LLC
Chambersburg PA
CBHW070255010526
44107CB00056B/2464
* 9 7 8 0 6 4 8 9 1 0 7 7 0 *